Brett Hale is a fifteen-year-old st███████████
ton, Victoria, Australia who has ███████████
rience working with a variety of ███████████
main interest in computers lies in w░░░░░g arcade games.
When not programming or studying, Brett has a wide
variety of other interests including playing tennis and
motorbike riding. Brett hopes to work as a computer
programmer in due course. He is the author of *Arcade
Games for Your Commodore 64* and *Arcade Games for
Your Vic 20*.

Also by Brett Hale

Arcade Games for Your Commodore 64
Arcade Games for Your Vic 20   .

and published by Corgi/Addison-Wesley

More Arcade Games for Your Commodore 64

Brett Hale

CORGI   ADDISON -WESLEY

MORE ARCADE GAMES FOR YOUR COMMODORE 64

A CORGI/ADDISON-WESLEY BOOK 0 552 99127 9

First publication in Great Britain

PRINTING HISTORY
Corgi/Addison-Wesley edition published 1984

This book is set in 11/12 Mallard

Corgi Books are published by Transworld Publishers Ltd., Century House, 61–63 Uxbridge Road, Ealing, London W5 5SA

Made and printed in West Germany by Mohndruck, Gütersloh

The programs presented in this book have been included for their instructional value. They have been tested with care but are not guaranteed for any particular purpose. The publisher does not offer any warranties or representations, nor does it accept any liabilities with respect to the programs.

Contents

Foreword

Brett Hale is an explorer. He's spent many, many hours searching out ways that BASIC can be used most effectively on the Commodore 64, and shares his discoveries with you in this book.

Brett has been exploring the potential of the 64 as an arcade games machine. You'll see when you get these great games up and running on your computer, that an awful lot can be achieved on the machine.

From *Galaxy Robbers*, through *Bullet Heads*, to *Nuclear Attack* you'll find a wide range of very exciting games to play with, and against, your computer. And best of all, because the games are in BASIC, you'll find it easy to modify and tailor the programs to put the stamp of your own personality on them.

Follow the lead of the explorer, and start genuine 'arcading'.

Tim Hartnell,
London, January, 1984

Tim Hartnell is the author of more than 30 books on microcomputers. Recent works include GAMES BBC COMPUTERS PLAY (Addison-Wesley/Interface, 1982), THE GIANT BOOK OF COMPUTER GAMES (Fontana, UK, 1983 and Ballantine, US, 1984) and PROGRAMMING YOUR ZX SPECTRUM (Interface, 1982).

ENCIRCLE

Now, here's a real challenge for you and your trusty 64. You have to try to get as many points as you can by driving your car around the screen, hitting the square, colored blocks. Different colored blocks are worth different points.

If you hit a border, or drive into your own trail, you'll lose a man. You start the game with five men.

Your controls are:
"I" to move up
"J" to move left
"K" to move right
"M" to move down

```
0 REM**ENCIRCLE**        JOYSTICK VERSION
1 V1=54296:W1=54276:A1=54277:H1=54273:
  H2=54272
2 POKEV1,15
5 POKE53281,0:POKE53290,2
6 DIMK(10),L(10):E=30
7 K(1)=3:K(2)=0:K(3)=4:K(5)=0:B=5
10 PRINT"◆":SC=1024:CL=55296
11 PRINT"█████████████████████████▚    █
    ◣      █      ◆      ◆      █      ◘      ▚      ◙
15 PRINT"█████████████████████████▚       ";
20 FORI=1TO10:X=INT(RND(1)*20)+1:Y=INT
   (RND(1)*17)+1:POKESC+X+40*Y,102
21 POKECL+X+40*Y,5
24 FORT=1TO50:NEXT
```

1

```
25 POKEA1,9:POKEW1,17
26 POKEH1,17:POKEH2,37:POKEW1,0
27 POKESC+X+40*Y,32
30 NEXT:POKESC+X+40*Y,102:POKECL+X+40
   *Y,5
40 X=X+1:IFPEEK(SC+X+40*Y)=102THEN3000
45 IFPEEK(SC+X+40*Y)=160THENGOSUB2000
46 IFX>39THEN3000
50 POKESC+X+40*Y,102:POKECL+X+40*Y,4:
   POKECL+X+40*Y,5
51 FORT=1TOE:NEXT
52 GOSUB1000
60 JV=PEEK(56320):JV=15-(JVAND15):IFJV=
   1THEN200
70 IFJV=4THEN100
80 IFJV=2THEN300
90 GOTO40
100 X=X-1:IFPEEK(SC+X+40*Y)=102THEN3000
105 IFPEEK(SC+X+40*Y)=160THENGOSUB2000
106 IFX<0THEN3000
110 POKESC+X+40*Y,102:POKECL+X+40*Y,4:
    POKECL+X+40*Y,5
111 FORT=1TOE:NEXT
112 GOSUB1000
120 JV=PEEK(56320):JV=15-(JVAND15):IFJV
    =1THEN200
130 IFJV=8THEN40
140 IFJV=2THEN300
150 GOTO100
200 Y=Y-1:IFPEEK(SC+X+40*Y)=102THEN3000
205 IFPEEK(SC+X+40*Y)=160THENGOSUB2000
206 IFY<1THEN3000
210 POKESC+X+40*Y,102:POKECL+X+40*Y,4:
    POKECL+X+40*Y,5
211 FORT=1TOE:NEXT
212 GOSUB1000
```

```
220 JV=PEEK(56320):JV=15-(JVAND15):
230 IFJV=8THEN40
240 IFJV=2THEN300
250 GOTO200
300 Y=Y+1:IFPEEK(SC+X+40*Y)=102THEN3000
305 IFPEEK(SC+X+40*Y)=160THENGOSUB2000
306 IFY>17THEN3000
310 POKESC+X+40*Y,102:POKECL+X+40*Y,4:
    POKECL+X+40*Y,5
311 FORT=1TOE:NEXT
312 GOSUB1000
320 JV=PEEK(56320):JV=15-(JVAND15):
    IFJV=4THEN100
330 IFJV=8THEN40
340 IFJV=1THEN200
350 GOTO300
1000 POKEA1,9:POKEW1,17:POKEH1,17:POKE
     H2,17:POKEW1,0
1001 IFW>10ANDW<500RW>50ANDW<1000RW>100
     ANDW<2000RW>200ANDW<2500RW>250ANDW
     <300THENE=E-5
1002 IFW>HTHENH=W
1003 PRINT"▧▧SCORE:"W"  HI:"H
1009 IFRND(1)<.87THENRETURN
1010 S=S+1:IFS>=10THENS=10:GOTO1030
1011 K(S)=INT(RND(1)*38)+1:L(S)=INT(RND
     (1)*17)+1
1020 POKESC+K(S)+40*L(S),160:POKECL+K(S)
     +40*L(S),INT(RND(1)*10)+1
1030 IFS<=0THENRETURN
1035 IFRND(1)<.88THENRETURN
1040 O=INT(RND(1)*S)+1:POKESC+K(O)+40*L
     (O),32:S=S-1:RETURN
2000 W=W+INT(RND(1)*20)
2070 POKEA1,9:POKEW1,17:FORT=200TO255:
```

```
      POKEW1,17:POKEH1,T:POKEH2,T:POKEW1,0:
      NEXT
2075  S=S-1
2080  RETURN
3000  POKEA1,9:POKEW1,17:FORT=128TO255
      STEP2:POKEW1,17:POKEH1,T:POKEH2,T
3010  POKEW1,0:NEXT
3020  B=B-1:IFB<=0THEN3040
3030  S=0:GETA$:GETA$:GOTO10
3040  FORT=1TO10:PRINT"SWWWWWWWWWW       
      JREGAME OVER"
3045  POKEA1,9:POKEW1,17:POKEH1,17:
      POKEH2,37:POKEW1,0
3050  FORG=1TO50:NEXTG
3060  PRINT"SWWWWWWWWWW       JREGAME
      OVER"
3065  POKEA1,9:POKEW1,17:POKEH1,15:POKE
      H2,35:POKEW1,0
3070  FORG=1TO50:NEXTG
3080  NEXT:POKE36876,0
3090  PRINT"VEANOTHER GAME?"
3100  GETA$:IFA$="N"THENEND
3110  IFA$<>"Y"THEN3100
3120  S=0:W=0:B=5:GOTO10

READY.
```

```
0  REM**ENCIRCLE**      KEYBOARD VERSION
1  V1=54296:W1=54276:A1=54277:H1=54273:
   H2=54272
2  POKEV1,15
5  POKE53281,0:POKE53280,2
```

```
6  DIMK(10),L(10):E=30
7  K(1)=3:K(2)=0:K(3)=4:K(5)=0:B=5
10 PRINT"◻":SC=1024:CL=55296
11 PRINT"▊▊▊▊▊▊▊▊▊▊▊▊▊▊▊▊▊▊▊▊▊▊◻▊   ▊      ◣
    ▓    █   ▀   ◪   ▢   ▚   ⊠    ";
15 PRINT"▊▊▊▊▊▊▊▊▊▊▊▊▊▊▊▊▊▊▊▊▊▊◻▊            "
20 FORI=1TO10:X=INT(RND(1)*20)+1:Y=INT
    (RND(1)*17)+1:POKESC+X+40*Y,102
21 POKECL+X+40*Y,5
24 FORT=1TO50:NEXT
25 POKEA1,9:POKEW1,17
26 POKEH1,17:POKEH2,37:POKEW1,0
27 POKESC+X+40*Y,32
30 NEXT:POKESC+X+40*Y,102:POKECL+X+40
    *Y,5
40 X=X+1:IFPEEK(SC+X+40*Y)=102THEN3000
45 IFPEEK(SC+X+40*Y)=160THENGOSUB2000
46 IFX>39THEN3000
50 POKESC+X+40*Y,102:POKECL+X+40*Y,4:
    POKECL+X+40*Y,5
51 FORT=1TOE:NEXT
52 GOSUB1000
60 GETA$:IFA$="I"THEN200
70 IFA$="J"THEN100
80 IFA$="M"THEN300
90 GOTO40
100 X=X-1:IFPEEK(SC+X+40*Y)=102THEN3000
105 IFPEEK(SC+X+40*Y)=160THENGOSUB2000
106 IFX<0THEN3000
110 POKESC+X+40*Y,102:POKECL+X+40*Y,4:
    POKECL+X+40*Y,5
111 FORT=1TOE:NEXT
112 GOSUB1000
120 GETA$:IFA$="I"THEN200
130 IFA$="K"THEN40
```

```
140  IFA$="M"THEN300
150  GOTO100
200  Y=Y-1:IFPEEK(SC+X+40*Y)=102THEN3000
205  IFPEEK(SC+X+40*Y)=160THENGOSUB2000
206  IFY<1THEN3000
210  POKESC+X+40*Y,102:POKECL+X+40*Y,4:
     POKECL+X+40*Y,5
211  FORT=1TOE:NEXT
212  GOSUB1000
220  GETA$:IFA$="J"THEN100
230  IFA$="K"THEN40
240  IFA$="M"THEN300
250  GOTO200
300  Y=Y+1:IFPEEK(SC+X+40*Y)=102THEN3000
305  IFPEEK(SC+X+40*Y)=160THENGOSUB2000
306  IFY>17THEN3000
310  POKESC+X+40*Y,102:POKECL+X+40*Y,4:
     POKECL+X+40*Y,5
311  FORT=1TOE:NEXT
312  GOSUB1000
320  GETA$:IFA$="J"THEN100
330  IFA$="K"THEN40
340  IFA$="I"THEN200
350  GOTO300
1000 POKEA1,9:POKEW1,17:POKEH1,17:POKE
     H2,17:POKEW1,0
1001 IFW>10ANDW<500RW>50ANDW<1000RW>100
     ANDW<2000RW>200ANDW<2500RW>250AND
     W<300THENE=E-5
1002 IFW>HTHENH=W
1003 PRINT"█████SCORE:"W"    HI:"H
1009 IFRND(1)<.87THENRETURN
1010 S=S+1:IFS>=10THENS=10:GOTO1030
1011 K(S)=INT(RND(1)*38)+1:L(S)=INT(RND
     (1)*17)+1
1020 POKESC+K(S)+40*L(S),160:POKECL+K(S)
```

```
        +40*L(S),INT(RND(1)*10)+1
1030  IFS<=0THENRETURN
1035  IFRND(1)<.88THENRETURN
1040  O=INT(RND(1)*S)+1:POKESC+K(O)+40*L
      (O),32:S=S-1:RETURN
2000  W=W+INT(RND(1)*20)
2070  POKEA1,9:POKEW1,17:FORT=200TO255:
      POKEW1,17:POKEH1,T:POKEH2,T:POKEW1,
      0:NEXT
2075  S=S-1
2080  RETURN
3000  POKEA1,9:POKEW1,17:FORT=128TO255
      STEP2:POKEW1,17:POKEH1,T:POKEH2,T
3010  POKEW1,0:NEXT
3020  B=B-1:IFB<=0THEN3040
3030  S=0:GETA$:GETA$:GOTO10
3040  FORT=1TO10:PRINT"█▒▒▒▒▒▒▒▒▒▒▒█████
      ███GAME OVER"
3045  POKEA1,9:POKEW1,17:POKEH1,17:POKE
      H2,37:POKEW1,0
3050  FORG=1TO50:NEXTG
3060  PRINT"█▒▒▒▒▒▒▒▒▒▒▒████████GAME
      OVER"
3065  POKEA1,9:POKEW1,17:POKEH1,15:POKE
      H2,35:POKEW1,0
3070  FORG=1TO50:NEXTG
3080  NEXT:POKE36876,0
3090  PRINT"▤◼ANOTHER GAME?"
3100  GETA$:IFA$="N"THENEND
3110  IFA$<>"Y"THEN3100
3120  S=0:W=0:B=5:GOTO10

READY.
```

FANTASY PINBALL

Take Tommy to task and prove your superiority.

Your ball comes out of the shoot as this game gets underway, and bounces over the screen, gaining points for you as it goes. If the ball comes in a straight line, you'll lose it.

You have to use your flippers to keep it in play for as long as possible. The ball will also vanish if it goes down the side shoot. You start the game with five balls.

The "Z" key raises your left flipper, and the "M" key raises the right one. Note that when playing the joystick version, pushing your joystick to the left will raise the left flipper, and pushing it to the right (naturally enough) will raise the right one.

```
0 REM**FANTASY PINBALL**
   JOYSTICK VERSION
1 V1=54296:W1=54276:A1=54272:H1=54273:
   H2=54272
5 POKE650,128:POKEV1,15
10 POKE53281,0:PRINT"◌":CO=54272
100 FORI=1024TO1904STEP40:POKEI,160:POKE
    I+CO,3:POKEI-18,160:POKEI-18+CO,3:NEXT
110 POKEI-20,160:POKEI-20+CO,3
120 FORI=1226TO1906STEP40:POKEI,93:POKE
    I+CO,3:POKEI-23,89:POKEI-23+CO,3
```

```
121 POKEI-41,35:POKEI-21,35:POKEI-22,
    35:POKEI-21+CO,0:POKEI-41+CO,0:NEXT
150 PRINT"▓▓                      "
160 PRINT"▓▓▓▓▓▓▓▓▓▓▓▓▓▓O░O░O░O░O▓▓▓▓▓▓▓▓▓▓↑
    ▬▬▓▓▓▓ 1 ▓ ▓▓▓▓▬▬▬▬";
170 PRINT"▓▓▓▓▓  ▓ ▓▓▓▓▓▓ 3 ▓ ▓▓▓▓▓▓  ▓ ▓"
180 PRINT"▓▓▓▓▓▓▓▓▓▓▓▓▓▓▓▓  ▓ ▓▓▓▓▓▓ 2 ▓
    ▓▓▓▓▓  ▓ ▓"
190 PRINT"▓▓▓▓▓▓▓▓▓▓▓▓▓▓▬▬▬▬▓▓▓▓▓ ▓*▓▓▓
    ▓▓▓▓▬▬▬▬"
200 PRINT"▓▓▓▓▓▓▓▓▓▓▓▓▓▓▓▓▓▓▓▓▓▓▓▓▓▓▓▬▬
    ▓▓▓▓▓ ▓*▓▓▓ ▓▓▓▓▬▬▬▬"
210 PRINT"▓▓▓▓▓▓▓▓▓▓▓▓▓▓▓▓▓▓▓▓▓▓▓▓▓Eo
    ▓▓▓▓▓▓▓▓▓▓▓▓o   o   o  "
211 PRINT"▓▓▓▓▓▓▓▓▓▓▓▓▓▓▓▓▓▓▓▓▓▓▓▓▓▓▓R▓     "
212 POKE1203,32:POKE1243,32:POKE1226,32
    :POKE1186,32
213 PRINT"▓▓▓▓▓▓▓▓"SPC(25)"F ▓A ▓N ▓T ▓A
    ▓S ▓Y"
214 PRINT:PRINTSPC(25)"P ▓I ▓N ▓B ▓A ▓L
    ▓L "
220 X=1885:E=-39
230 FORI=1TO20
250 POKEX,81:POKEX+CO,4
260 FORI1=1TO60:NEXT
270 POKEX,35:POKEX+CO,0:X=X-40
280 IFI>=18THENPOKEX,32
290 NEXT
300 X=X-E:IFPEEK(X)=32THEN310
302 IFX>1964THEN4030
303 IFKK=0ANDRND(1)>.7THENGOSUB5000
304 IFKK=1ANDRND(1)>.7THENGOSUB5050
305 GOSUB1000
310 POKEX,81:POKEX+CO,4
330 JV=PEEK(56320):JV=15-(JVAND15)
```

```
370  IFJV=0THENPOKE1911,64:POKE1912,70:
     POKE1913,82:LL=3
371  IFJV=0THENPOKE1911+CO,1:POKE1912+CO,
     1:POKE1913+CO,1
380  IFJV=0THENPOKE1917,82:POKE1918,70:
     POKE1919,64
381  IFJV=0THENPOKE1917+CO,1:POKE1918+CO,
     1:POKE1919+CO,1
390  POKE1914,32:POKE1915,32:POKE1916,32
400  IFJV=4THENPOKE1911,67:POKE1912,67:
     POKE1913,67
401  IFJV=4THENPOKE1911+CO,1:POKE1912+CO
     ,1:POKE1913+CO,1
410  IFJV=8THENPOKE1917,67:POKE1918,67:
     POKE1919,67
411  IFJV=8THENPOKE1917+CO,1:POKE1918+CO
     ,1:POKE1919+CO,1
412  IFX>1910ANDX<1920ANDLL=3THEN4030
590  POKEX,32
600  GOTO300
1000 P=PEEK(X):L=PEEK(X+CO)
1001 POKEX,P:POKEX+CO,L
1002 IFP=67ANDE=-41THENE=39:X=X-1:IFRND
     (1)>.6THENX=X+2
1003 IFP=67ANDE=-39THENE=41:X=X+1:IFRND
     (1)>.6THENX=X-2
1004 IFP=67ANDE=-40THENE=41:X=X-1:IFRND
     (1)>.6THENX=X+2
1005 IFX>1911ANDX<1920ANDP<>67THEN4030
1006 IFP=160ANDE=-40THENE=41
1010 IFP=98ANDE=-41THENE=39:W=200:S=S+20
1011 IFP=87THEN3000:W=220
1012 IFP=35THEN4000
1020 IFP=98ANDE=-39THENE=41:S=S+20
1025 IFP=90THENS=S+200:W=200
```

```
1030  IFP=97ANDE=39THENE=41:W=214:S=S+30
1040  IFP=97ANDE=-41THENE=-39:S=S+30
1050  IFP=225ANDE=-39THENE=-41:W=190:S=S
      +100
1060  IFP=225ANDE=41THENE=39:S=S+100
1070  IFP=226ANDE=41THENE=-39:W=210:S=S
      +100
1080  IFP=226ANDE=39THENE=-41:S=S+100
1090  IFP=160ANDE=39THENE=41:W=225:S=S+5
1100  IFP=160ANDE=-41THENE=-39:S=S+5
1110  IFP=160ANDE=41THENE=39:S=S+5
1120  IFP=160ANDE=-39THENE=-41:S=S+5
1121  IFE=39ANDP=89THENE=41:W=228:S=S+5
1122  IFE=-41ANDP=89THENE=-39:S=S+5
1123  IFE=41ANDP=93THENE=39:W=204:S=S+5
1124  IFE=-39ANDP=93THENE=-41:S=S+5
1130  IFX<1064ANDE=39THENE=-41
1131  IFX<1064ANDE=41THENE=-39
1150  IFX>1904ANDE=-39THENE=41
1160  IFX>1904ANDE=-41THENE=39
1165  IFS>HTHENH=S
1170  PRINT"▆▆ SCORE:"S"   HI:"H
1200  L=PEEK(X+CO)
1210  X=X-E:IFPEEK(X)<>32THEN1000
1211  POKEX,P:POKEX+CO,L
1220  POKEA1,9:POKEW1,17:POKEH1,W:POKEH2,
      W:POKEW1,0
1230  RETURN
3000  FORW=128TO255STEP2:POKEW1,17:POKE
      H1,W:POKEH2,W:POKEW1,0:NEXT
3001  FORW=255TO128STEP-4:POKEW1,17:POKE
      H1,W:POKEH2,W:POKEW1,0:NEXT
3009  O=INT(RND(1)*5)+1
3010  IFO=1THENE=41
3015  S=S+INT(RND(1)*300)+1
3020  IFO=2THENE=39
```

```
3030 IFO=3THENE=-39
3040 IFO=4THENE=-41
3050 IFO=5THENE=-40
3060 GOTO1020
4000 FORT=XTO1904STEP40:POKET,81:POKET+
     CO,4:FORI1=1TO60:NEXTI1:POKET,32:NEXT
4030 W1=54290:A1=54291:H1=54287:H2=54286
     :POKEA1,9
4031 FORYG=128TO0STEP-7:POKEW1,17:POKE
     H1,YG:POKEH2,YG:POKEW1,0
4032 FORGY=1TO30:NEXT:NEXT
4040 Q=Q+1:LL=0:IFQ=5THEN4050
4045 W1=54276:A1=54277:H1=54273:H2=54272
     :GOTO5
4050 PRINT"◼◼◼"SPC(23)"ANOTHER GO?"
4060 GETA$:IFA$="N"THEN4080
4065 IFA$<>"Y"THEN4060
4070 S=0:Q=0:GOTO5
4080 POKE54278,0:POKE54273,0:POKE54272,
     0:POKE54276,0:POKE54277,0:PRINT"◼◼◼"
4090 POKE53281,6:END
5000 KK=1
5010 PRINT"◼◼◼◼◼◼◼◼◼◼◼◼◼◼◼◼◼◼◼◼◼          "
5020 PRINT"◼◼◼◼◼◼◼              "
5030 PRINT"◼◼◼◼◼◼◼              "
5040 RETURN
5050 KK=0
5060 PRINT"◼◼◼◼◼◼◼◼◼◼◼◼◼◼◼◼◼◼◼◼◼__ __"
5070 PRINT"◼◼◼◼◼◼◼ ◼*◼◼◼ ◼    ◼◼*◼◼ "
5080 PRINT"◼◼◼◼◼◼◼◼__◼      ◼__◼"
5090 RETURN

READY.
```

_____

14

```
0 REM**FANTASY PINBALL**
  KEYBOARD VERSION
1 V1=54296:W1=54276:A1=54272:H1=54273:
  H2=54272
5 POKE650,128:POKEV1,15
10 POKE53281,0:PRINT"◻":CO=54272
100 FORI=1024TO1904STEP40:POKEI,160:POKE
    I+CO,3:POKEI-18,160:POKEI-18+CO,3:NEXT
110 POKEI-20,160:POKEI-20+CO,3
120 FORI=1226TO1906STEP40:POKEI,93:POKE
    I+CO,3:POKEI-23,89:POKEI-23+CO,3
121 POKEI-41,35:POKEI-21,35:POKEI-22,35
    :POKEI-21+CO,0:POKEI-41+CO,0:NEXT
150 PRINT"▓▒▲                           "
160 PRINT"▓▓░░░░░░░░░░▓▓◻▓◻▓◻▓◻▓◻▓░░░░░▓▓▓▓▓◻
    ▓▓▓▓▓1▓▓▓▓▓▓▓▄";
170 PRINT"◻▓▓▓▄  ▓▓ ▓▓▓▓▓3▓▓ ▓▓▓▓▓  ▓▓ ▓"
180 PRINT"▓▓░░░░░░░▓▓▓▓▓  ▓▓ ▓▓▓▓▓2▓▓
    ▓▓▓▓▓  ▓▓ ▓"
190 PRINT"▓░░░░░▓▓▓▓▓▓▓▓▄▄▄▓▓▓▓▓ ▓*▓▓▓▓
    ▓▓▓▓▄▄▄▄"
200 PRINT"▓▓░░░░░░░░░░░░░░░▓▓▓▓▓▓▓▓▓▓▓▓▓▓▓▓
    ▄▄▄▓▓▓▓ ▓*▓▓▓ ▓▓▓▄▄▄▄"
210 PRINT"▓▓░░░░░░░░░░░░░░░▓▓▓▓▓▓▓▓▓▓◻O
    ▓░░░░░░░▓▓▓▓O   O   O   "
211 PRINT"▓▓░░░░░░░░░░░░░░░░░░░░░░░░░░░░▓▲    "
212 POKE1203,32:POKE1243,32:POKE1226,32:
    POKE1186,32
213 PRINT"▓▓░░░░░░░"SPC(25)"F ░A ░N ░T ░A
    ░S ░Y"
214 PRINT:PRINTSPC(25)"P ▓I ▓N ▓B ░A ░L
    ░L"
220 X=1885:E=-39
230 FORI=1TO20
250 POKEX,81:POKEX+CO,4
```

15

```
260 FORI1=1TO60:NEXT
270 POKEX,35:POKEX+CO,0:X=X-40
280 IFI>=18THENPOKEX,32
290 NEXT
300 X=X-E:IFPEEK(X)=32THEN310
302 IFX>1964THEN4030
303 IFKK=0ANDRND(1)>.7THENGOSUB5000
304 IFKK=1ANDRND(1)>.7THENGOSUB5050
305 GOSUB1000
310 POKEX,81:POKEX+CO,4
330 GETA$
370 IFA$=" "THENPOKE1911,64:POKE1912,70
    :POKE1913,82:LL=3
371 IFA$=" "THENPOKE1911+CO,1:POKE1912
    +CO,1:POKE1913+CO,1
380 IFA$=" "THENPOKE1917,82:POKE1918,70:
    POKE1919,64
381 IFA$=" "THENPOKE1917+CO,1:POKE1918
    +CO,1:POKE1919+CO,1
390 POKE1914,32:POKE1915,32:POKE1916,32
400 IFA$="Z"THENPOKE1911,67:POKE1912,67
    :POKE1913,67
401 IFA$="Z"THENPOKE1911+CO,1:POKE1912
    +CO,1:POKE1913+CO,1
410 IFA$="M"THENPOKE1917,67:POKE1918,67
    :POKE1919,67
411 IFA$="M"THENPOKE1917+CO,1:POKE1918
    +CO,1:POKE1919+CO,1
412 IFX>1910ANDX<1920ANDLL=3THEN4030
590 POKEX,32
600 GOTO300
1000 P=PEEK(X):L=PEEK(X+CO)
1001 POKEX,P:POKEX+CO,L
1002 IFP=67ANDE=-41THENE=39:X=X-1:IFRND
     (1)>.6THENX=X+2
1003 IFP=67ANDE=-39THENE=41:X=X+1:IFRND
```

```
      (1)>.6THENX=X-2
1004  IFP=67ANDE=-40THENE=41:X=X-1:IFRND
      (1)>.6THENX=X+2
1005  IFX>1911ANDX<1920ANDP<>67THEN4030
1006  IFP=160ANDE=-40THENE=41
1010  IFP=98ANDE=-41THENE=39:W=200:S=S+20
1011  IFP=87THEN3000:W=220
1012  IFP=35THEN4000
1020  IFP=98ANDE=-39THENE=41:S=S+20
1025  IFP=90THENS=S+200:W=200
1030  IFP=97ANDE=39THENE=41:W=214:S=S+30
1040  IFP=97ANDE=-41THENE=-39:S=S+30
1050  IFP=225ANDE=-39THENE=-41:W=190:S=S
      +100
1060  IFP=225ANDE=41THENE=39:S=S+100
1070  IFP=226ANDE=41THENE=-39:W=210:S=S
      +100
1080  IFP=226ANDE=39THENE=-41:S=S+100
1090  IFP=160ANDE=39THENE=41:W=225:S=S+5
1100  IFP=160ANDE=-41THENE=-39:S=S+5
1110  IFP=160ANDE=41THENE=39:S=S+5
1120  IFP=160ANDE=-39THENE=-41:S=S+5
1121  IFE=39ANDP=89THENE=41:W=228:S=S+5
1122  IFE=-41ANDP=89THENE=-39:S=S+5
1123  IFE=41ANDP=93THENE=39:W=204:S=S+5
1124  IFE=-39ANDP=93THENE=-41:S=S+5
1130  IFX<1064ANDE=39THENE=-41
1131  IFX<1064ANDE=41THENE=-39
1150  IFX>1904ANDE=-39THENE=41
1160  IFX>1904ANDE=-41THENE=39
1165  IFS>HTHENH=S
1170  PRINT"▓▓ SCORE:"S"   HI:"H
1200  L=PEEK(X+CO)
1210  X=X-E:IFPEEK(X)<>32THEN1000
1211  POKEX,P:POKEX+CO,L
```

```
1220  POKEA1,9:POKEW1,17:POKEH1,W:POKE
      H2,W:POKEW1,0
1230  RETURN
3000  FORW=128TO255STEP2:POKEW1,17:POKE
      H1,W:POKEH2,W:POKEW1,0:NEXT
3001  FORW=255TO128STEP-4:POKEW1,17:POKE
      H1,W:POKEH2,W:POKEW1,0:NEXT
3009  O=INT(RND(1)*5)+1
3010  IFO=1THENE=41
3015  S=S+INT(RND(1)*300)+1
3020  IFO=2THENE=39
3030  IFO=3THENE=-39
3040  IFO=4THENE=-41
3050  IFO=5THENE=-40
3060  GOTO1020
4000  FORT=XTO1904STEP40:POKET,81:POKE
      T+CO,4:FORI1=1TO60:NEXTI1:POKET,32:
      NEXT
4030  W1=54290:A1=54291:H1=54287:H2=54286
      :POKEA1,9
4031  FORYG=128TO0STEP-7:POKEW1,17:POKE
      H1,YG:POKEH2,YG:POKEW1,0
4032  FORGY=1TO30:NEXT:NEXT
4040  Q=Q+1:LL=0:IFQ=5THEN4050
4045  W1=54276:A1=54277:H1=54273:H2=54272
      :GOTO5.
4050  PRINT"███"SPC(23)"ANOTHER GO?"
4060  GETA$:IFA$="N"THEN4080
4065  IFA$<>"Y"THEN4060
4070  S=0:Q=0:GOTO5
4080  POKE54278,0:POKE54273,0:POKE54272,
      0:POKE54276,0:POKE54277,0:PRINT"███"
4090  POKE53281,6:END
5000  KK=1
5010  PRINT"███████████████████████      "
5020  PRINT"██████████              "
```

18

```
5030 PRINT"██████                    "
5040 RETURN
5050 KK=0
5060 PRINT"███████████████████████████████ ████"
5070 PRINT"███████ ██*██ █    █ ██*██ "
5080 PRINT"███████R____█      ▄____█"
5090 RETURN
```

READY.

SPEEDY BOULDERS

Strange objects inhabit the world of Commodore 64 arcade games, and the Speedy Boulders are no exception.

In this action-packed dazzler, you have to fire the ship's laser at the asteroids as they move closer and closer to your ship.

If things get too hot for comfort, you can trigger your Hyperspace Option. You're allowed to do this eleven times in a game. A less dramatic way of getting out of the way of an asteroid is to thrust forwards.

You lose a man each time an asteroid hits your ship. You have three lives in all.

Here are your controls:
"J" – rotates you anti-clockwise
"K" – rotates you clockwise
"I" – thrusts you forwards
"H" – to trigger the Hyperspace Option
Space bar – to fire your laser

In the joystick version, you push the joystick up for forward thrust, and press the fire button to trigger your laser.

```
5 REM**SPEEDY BOULDERS**JOYSTICK VERSION
10 V1=54296:W1=54276:H1=54273:H2=54272
```

21

```
50 C=113:L=7:POKE650,255
60 PRINT"◰":POKE53281,0:SC=1024:CO=54272:
   CL=55296:X=20:Y=12
70 FORI=1TO7:Q(I)=1024+INT(RND(1)*1000):
   NEXT
80 FORI=1TO7:W(I)=INT((RND(1)*3)+39):
   IFRND(1)>.6THENW(I)=-W(I)
90 NEXT
100 POKESC+X+40*Y,32
110 JV=PEEK(56320):FR=JVAND16:
    JV=15-(JVAND15):GETA$:IFJV=8THENA=A+1
120 IFA$="H"ANDV<11THENX=INT(RND(1)*38)+1
    :Y=INT(RND(1)*20)+1:V=V+1
140 IFJV=1THEN620
150 IFJV=4THENA=A-1
160 IFA=1THENC=113
170 IFA=2THENC=107
180 IFA=3THENC=114
190 IFA=4THENC=115
200 IFA<1THENA=4:C=115
210 IFA>4THENA=1:C=113
211 IFTT=0ANDRND(1)>.8THENTT=1
212 IFTT=0THEN220
213 PP=1064+HH:POKEPP,32:POKEPP+1,32:
    POKEPP+2,32
214 HH=HH+1:IFHH=38THENHH=0:TT=0
215 PP=1064+HH:POKEPP,86:POKEPP+1,90:
    POKEPP+2,86:POKEPP+CO,8:POKEPP+CO+1,3
216 POKEPP+CO+2,8
220 POKESC+X+40*Y,C:POKECL+X+40*Y,1
230 IFFR=0THEN380
240 FORI=1TO7:IFQ(I)=0THEN370
250 POKEQ(I),32
270 Q(I)=Q(I)+W(I)
```

22

```
280  IFQ(I)<1024THENQ(I)=Q(I)+1001
290  IFQ(I)>2023THENQ(I)=Q(I)-999
300  POKEQ(I),81:POKEQ(I)+CO,I
310  IFQ(I)<>SC+X+40*YTHEN370
320  POKE53281,2:POKE54278,240:POKE54277,9
330  MM=MM+1:FORT=15TO0STEP-1:POKEW1,129:
     POKEH1,40:POKEH2,200:POKEV1,T:
     POKEW1,0
331  NEXT:POKEHH1,0:POKEH2,0:POKEV1,15
340  IFMM=3THENPRINT"█████SCORE:"H*10:END
350  FORG=1TO1000:NEXT
360  H=H+L:S=0:GOTO60
370  NEXT
371  IFTT=1ANDTT(1)=0ANDRND(1)>.
     7THENGOSUB5000
372  IFTT(1)=0THEN379
373  POKEAA,32:AA=AA+SS:IFPEEK(AA)<>32
     THENGOSUB5050
374  POKEAA,90:POKEAA+CO,3
375  IFAA>SC+X+40*YTHENTT(1)=0:POKEAA,32
379  GOTO100
380  POKEA1,9:POKEV1,15:FORT=128TO255STEP
     8:POKEW1,17:POKEH1,T:POKEW1,0:NEXT
390  IFC=113THEN430
400  IFC=114THEN460
410  IFC=107THEN490
420  IFC=115THEN520
430  FORR=YTO1STEP-1:P=PEEK(SC+X+40*R):
     IFP=81THEN550
431  IFP=90ORP=86THENH=H+INT(RND(1)*200)
     +1:POKEPP,32:POKEPP+1,32:POKEPP+2,32
432  IFP=90ORP=86THENHH=0:TT=0:POKEAA,
     32:AA=0:SS=0:TT(1)=0
440  P=SC+X+40*R:POKEP,93:POKEP+40,32:
     POKEP+CO,7:NEXT
```

23

```
450 POKESC+X+40*(R+1),32:GOTO240
    THEN550
460 FORR=YTO23:P=PEEK(SC+X+40*R):IFP=81
461 IFP=90ORP=86THENH=H+INT(RND(1)*200)
    +1:POKEPP,32:POKEPP+1,32:POKEPP+2,32
462 IFP=90ORP=86THENHH=0:TT=0:POKEAA,32:
    AA=0:SS=0:TT(1)=0
470 P=SC+X+40*R:POKEP,93:POKEP-40,32:
    POKEP+CO,7:NEXT
480 POKESC+X+40*(R-1),32:GOTO240
490 FORR=XTO39:P=PEEK(SC+R+40*Y):IFP=81
    THEN550
491 IFP=90ORP=86THENH=H+INT(RND(1)*200)
    +1:POKEPP,32:POKEPP+1,32:POKEPP+2,32
492 IFP=90ORP=86THENHH=0:TT=0:POKEAA,32:
    AA=0:SS=0:TT(1)=0
510 POKESC+(R-1)+40*Y,32:GOTO240
520 FORR=XTO2STEP-1:P=PEEK(SC+R+40*Y):
    IFP=81THEN550
521 IFP=90ORP=86THENH=H+INT(RND(1)*200)
    +1:POKEPP,32:POKEPP+1,32:POKEPP+2,32
522 IFP=90ORP=86THENHH=0:TT=0:POKEAA,32:
    AA=0:SS=0:TT(1)=0
530 P=SC+R+40*Y:POKEP,64:POKEP+1,32:
    POKEP+CO,7:NEXT
540 POKESC+(R+1)+40*Y,32:GOTO240
550 IFC=113ORC=114THEN555
551 P=SC+R+40*Y:POKEP,160:POKEP+39,255:
    POKEP+41,127:POKEP-39,255:POKEP-41,
    127
552 POKEP+CO,5:POKEP+39+CO,2:POKEP+41+CO
    ,2:POKEP-39+CO,2:POKEP-41+CO,2
553 GOTO560
```

```
555 P=SC+X+40*R:POKEP,160:POKEP+39,255:
    POKEP+41,127:POKEP-39,255:POKEP-41,
    127
556 POKEP+CO,5:POKEP+39+CO,5:POKEP+41+CO
    ,5:POKEP-39+CO,5:POKEP-41+CO,5
560 POKE53281,0:FORT1=1TO40:NEXT
570 POKE54278,240:POKE54277,9
571 FORT=15TO0STEP-1:POKEW1,129:POKEH1,
    40:POKEH2,200:POKEV1,T:POKEW1,0
572 NEXT:POKEHH1,0:POKEH2,0:POKEV1,15
580 FORI=1TO7:IFSC+X+40*R=Q(I)ORSC+R+40
    *Y=Q(I)THENPOKEQ(I),32:Q(I)=0:W(I)
    =0:S=S+1
590 IFS=LTHENS=0:H=H+L:GOTO60
591 IFC=113ORC=114THEN594
592 P=SC+R+40*Y:POKEP,32:POKEP+39,32:
    POKEP+41,32:POKEP-39,32:POKEP-41,32
593 POKEP+1,32:POKEP-1,32:GOTO600
594 P=SC+X+40*R:POKEP,32:POKEP+39,32:
    POKEP+41,32:POKEP-39,32:POKEP-41,32
595 POKEP+40,32:POKEP-40,32
600 NEXT
610 GOTO240
620 IFC=115THENX=X-2
630 IFC=114THENY=Y+2
640 IFC=107THENX=X+2
650 IFC=113THENY=Y-2
660 IFY<1THENY=23
670 IFY>23THENY=1
680 IFX<1THENX=39
690 IFX>39THENX=1
700 GOTO150
5000 AA=HH+1+1064:SS=INT(RND(1)*3+39):
     TT(1)=1
5010 RETURN
```

```
5050 PO=PEEK(AA):IFPO<>107ANDPO<>113
     ANDPO<>114ANDPO<>115THENGOTO374
5060 GOTO320
```

READY.

```
5 REM**SPEEDY BOULDERS**KEYBOARD VERSION
10 V1=54296:W1=54276:H1=54273:H2=54272
50 C=113:L=7:POKE650,255
60 PRINT"⬛":POKE53281,0:SC=1024:CO=54272
   :CL=55296:X=20:Y=12
70 FORI=1TO7:Q(I)=1024+INT(RND(1)*1000)
   :NEXT
80 FORI=1TO7:W(I)=INT((RND(1)*3)+39):
   IFRND(1)>.6THENW(I)=-W(I)
90 NEXT
100 POKESC+X+40*Y,32
110 GETA$:IFA$="K"THENA=A+1
120 IFA$="H"ANDV<11THENX=INT(RND(1)*38)
    +1:Y=INT(RND(1)*20)+1:V=V+1
140 IFA$="I"THEN620
150 IFA$="J"THENA=A-1
160 IFA=1THENC=113
170 IFA=2THENC=107
180 IFA=3THENC=114
190 IFA=4THENC=115
200 IFA<1THENA=4:C=115
210 IFA>4THENA=1:C=113
211 IFTT=0ANDRND(1)>.8THENTT=1
212 IFTT=0THEN220
213 PP=1064+HH:POKEPP,32:PQKEPP+1,32:
    POKEPP+2,32
```

```
214 HH=HH+1:IFHH=38THENHH=0:TT=0
215 PP=1064+HH:POKEPP,86:POKEPP+1,90:
    POKEPP+2,86:POKEPP+CO,8:POKEPP+CO+1,3
216 POKEPP+CO+2,8
220 POKESC+X+40*Y,C:POKECL+X+40*Y,1
230 IFA$=" "THEN380
240 FORI=1TO7:IFQ(I)=0THEN370
250 POKEQ(I),32
270 Q(I)=Q(I)+W(I)
280 IFQ(I)<1024THENQ(I)=Q(I)+1001
290 IFQ(I)>2023THENQ(I)=Q(I)-999
300 POKEQ(I),81:POKEQ(I)+CO,I
310 IFQ(I)<>SC+X+40*YTHEN370
320 POKE53281,2:POKE54278,240:POKE
    54277,9
330 MM=MM+1:FORT=15TO0STEP-1:POKEW1,129
    :POKEH1,40:POKEH2,200:POKEV1,T:POKE
    W1,0
331 NEXT:POKEHH1,0:POKEH2,0:POKEV1,15
340 IFMM=3THENPRINT"    SCORE:"H*10:END
350 FORG=1TO1000:NEXT
360 H=H+L:S=0:GOTO60
370 NEXT
371 IFTT=1ANDTT(1)=0ANDRND(1)>.7THEN
    GOSUB5000
372 IFTT(1)=0THEN379
373 POKEAA,32:AA=AA+SS:IFPEEK(AA)<>32
    THENGOSUB5050
374 POKEAA,90:POKEAA+CO,3
375 IFAA>SC+X+40*YTHENTT(1)=0:POKEAA,32
379 GOTO100
380 POKEA1,9:POKEV1,15:FORT=128TO255STEP
    8:POKEW1,17:POKEH1,T:POKEW1,0:NEXT
390 IFC=113THEN430
400 IFC=114THEN460
```

```
410  IFC=107THEN490
420  IFC=115THEN520
430  FORR=YTO1STEP-1:P=PEEK(SC+X+40*R):
     IFP=81THEN550
431  IFP=90ORP=86THENH=H+INT(RND(1)*200)
     +1:POKEPP,32:POKEPP+1,32:POKEPP+2,32
432  IFP=90ORP=86THENHH=0:TT=0:POKEAA,32
     :AA=0:SS=0:TT(1)=0
440  P=SC+X+40*R:POKEP,93:POKEP+40,32:
     POKEP+CO,7:NEXT
450  POKESC+X+40*(R+1),32:GOTO240
460  FORR=YTO23:P=PEEK(SC+X+40*R):IFP=81
     THEN550
461  IFP=90ORP=86THENH=H+INT(RND(1)*200)
     +1:POKEPP,32:POKEPP+1,32:POKEPP+2,32
462  IFP=90ORP=86THENHH=0:TT=0:POKEAA,32
     :AA=0:SS=0:TT(1)=0
470  P=SC+X+40*R:POKEP,93:POKEP-40,32:
     POKEP+CO,7:NEXT
480  POKESC+X+40*(R-1),32:GOTO240
490  FORR=XTO39:P=PEEK(SC+R+40*Y):IFF=81
     THEN550
491  IFP=90ORP=86THENH=H+INT(RND(1)*200)
     +1:POKEPP,32:POKEPP+1,32:POKEPP+2,32
492  IFP=90ORP=86THENHH=0:TT=0:POKEAA,32
     :AA=0:SS=0:TT(1)=0
500  P=SC+R+40*Y:POKEP,64:POKEP-1,32:
     POKEP+CO,7:NEXT
510  POKESC+(R-1)+40*Y,32:GOTO240
520  FORR=XTO2STEP-1:P=PEEK(SC+R+40*Y):
     IFP=81THEN550
521  IFP=90ORP=86THENH=H+INT(RND(1)*200)
     +1:POKEPP,32:POKEPP+1,32:POKEPP+2,32
522  IFP=90ORP=86THENHH=0:TT=0:POKEAA,32:
     AA=0:SS=0:TT(1)=0
```

```
530 P=SC+R+40*Y:POKEP,64:POKEP+1,32:
    POKEP+CO,7:NEXT
540 POKESC+(R+1)+40*Y,32:GOTO240
550 IFC=113ORC=114THEN555
551 P=SC+R+40*Y:POKEP,160:POKEP+39,255
    :POKEP+41,127:POKEP-39,255:POKEP-41,
    127
552 POKEP+CO,5:POKEP+39+CO,2:POKEP+41+CO
    ,2:POKEP-39+CO,2:POKEP-41+CO,2
553 GOTO560
555 P=SC+X+40*R:POKEP,160:POKEP+39,255:
    POKEP+41,127:POKEP-39,255:POKEP-41,
    127
556 POKEP+CO,5:POKEP+39+CO,5:POKEP+41
    +CO,5:POKEP-39+CO,5:POKEP-41+CO,5
560 POKE53281,0:FORT1=1TO40:NEXT
570 POKE54278,240:POKE54277,9
571 FORT=15TO0STEP-1:POKEW1,129:POKEH1,
    40:POKEH2,200:POKEV1,T:POKEW1,0
572 NEXT:POKEHH1,0:POKEH2,0:POKEV1,15
580 FORI=1TO7:IFSC+X+40*R=Q(I)ORSC+R+40
    *Y=Q(I)THENPOKEQ(I),32:Q(I)=0:W(I)=0
    :S=S+1
590 IFS=LTHENS=0:H=H+L:GOTO60
591 IFC=113ORC=114THEN594
592 P=SC+R+40*Y:POKEP,32:POKEP+39,32:
    POKEP+41,32:POKEP-39,32:POKEP-41,32
593 POKEP+1,32:POKEP-1,32:GOTO600
594 P=SC+X+40*R:POKEP,32:POKEP+39,32:
    POKEP+41,32:POKEP-39,32:POKEP-41,32
595 POKEP+40,32:POKEP-40,32
600 NEXT
610 GOTO240
620 IFC=115THENX=X-2
630 IFC=114THENY=Y+2
```

```
640  IFC=107THENX=X+2
650  IFC=113THENY=Y-2
660  IFY<1THENY=23
670  IFY>23THENY=1
680  IFX<1THENX=39
690  IFX>39THENX=1
700  GOTO150
5000 AA=HH+1+1064:SS=INT(RND(1)*3+39)
     :TT(1)=1
5010 RETURN
5050 PO=PEEK(AA):IFPO<>107ANDPO<>113AND
     PO<>114ANDPO<>115THENGOTO374
5060 GOTO320

READY.
```

NUCLEAR ATTACK

Nuclear missiles from another planet are penetrating your defence field.

In this game, you move your sights around the screen, and fire your guns in an attempt to destroy the missiles. If you stop the missiles, you'll get an extra man (and more nuclear missiles will be sent). The game will end when seven towns have been destroyed.

In the keyboard version, you use the following controls:
"I" – to move up
"J" – to move left
"K" – to move right
"M" – to move down
Space bar – to fire your missiles

```
0 REM**NUCLEAR ATTACK** JOYSTICK VERSION
1 V1=54296:A1=54277:W1=54276:H1=54273:
  H2=54272
5 POKE6 0,255
10 POKE53281,0:PRINT"    SKILL LEVEL
   (1-6)"
11 PRINT:PRINT"  LEVEL  6=  'PRO '"
12 PRINT:PRINT"LEVEL  1=  'AMATEUR '"
20 INPUTL
21 IFL=1THEND=20
22 IFL=2THEND=6
23 IFL=3THEND=5
24 IFL=4THEND=3
```

32

```
25  IFL=5THEND=2
26  IFL=6THEND=0:L=5
29  PRINT"◌"
30  IFL<1ORL>6THEN10
40  X=20:Y=19:SC=1024:CO=54272:CL=55296
50  A(1)=1024:A(2)=1034:A(3)=1044:A(4)=
    1054:A(5)=1060
55  FORT=1TO100:LL=INT(RND(1)*1000):POKE
    SC+LL,46:POKECL+LL,1:NEXT
56  FORI=1904TO1943:POKEI,160:POKEI+CO,2
    :NEXT
57  PRINT"◙◙◙◙◙◙◙◙◙◙◙◙◙◙◙◙◙◙◙◙◙◙◙◙◙◙◙◙▚      ▧ ▆
    ▧ ▆    ▧ ▆    ▧    ▆◌▆▆▆▆R ▆"
58  PRINTSPC(26)"▚ ▆       ▧ ▆     ▧ ▆"
60  FORI=1TOL:IFA(I)=0THEN130
61  IFI=6THEN60
62  A(I)=A(I)+INT(RND(1)*3+39)
63  IFA(I)>1806THEN1000
64  IFA(I)>1904THEN1000
70  POKEA(I),102:POKEA(I)+CO,I
71  FORU=1TOD*10:NEXT
75  POKESC+X+40*Y,32
76  PRINT"◙◙◙SCORE:"SS*10;" HITS:"H
80  JV=PEEK(56320):FR=JVAND16:JV=15-
    (JVAND15):IFJV=1THENY=Y-2
90  IFJV=4THENX=X-2
100 IFJV=8THENX=X+2
110 IFJV=2THENY=Y+2
111 IFFR=0THEN300
120 POKESC+X+40*Y,91:POKECL+X+40*Y,4
130 NEXT:GOTO60
300 POKEV1,15:POKEA1,9:FORM=128TO255STEP
    5:POKEW1,17:POKEH1,M:POKEH2,M:POKE
    W1,0
301 NEXT
310 FORM1=1TO15:NEXTM1
```

33

```basic
400 P=SC+X+40*Y
401 POKEP-40,79:POKEP-39,80:POKEP+40,76
    :POKEP+41,122:POKEP,101:POKEP+1,103
402 P=CL+X+40*Y
403 POKEP-40,1:POKEP-39,1:POKEP+40,1:
    POKEP+41,1:POKEP,1:POKEP+1,1
404 FORU1=1TO80:NEXT:P=SC+X+40*Y
405 POKEP-40,32:POKEP-39,32:POKEP+40,32
    :POKEP+41,32:POKEP,32:POKEP+1,32
410 POKEP-41,85:POKEP-40,64:POKEP-39,73
    :POKEP-1,93:POKEP+1,93:POKEP+39,74:
     POKEP+40,64
411 P=CL+X+40*Y
413 POKEP-41,1:POKEP-40,1:POKEP-39,1:
    POKEP-1,1:POKEP+1,1:POKEP+21,1:
    POKEP+40,1
420 POKEP+41,1
421 P=SC+X+40*Y
430 FORZ=1TOL:O=A(Z)
440 IFO=P-41ORO=P-400RO=P-390RO=P-10RO
    =P+10RO=P+390RO=P+400RO=P+41THEN
     A(Z)=0:S=S+1
441 IFS=LTHENH=H-1:SS=SS+INT(RND(1)*200)
    +1:D=D-1:GOTO2505
450 NEXT
451 POKEP-41,32:POKEP-40,32:POKEP-39,32:
    POKEP-1,32:POKEP+1,32:POKEP+39,32
    :POKEP+40,32
452 POKEP+41,32
500 GOTO60
1000 POKE54278,240:POKEH1,40:POKEH2,200:
     POKEW1,129:FORYG=15TO0STEP-1:POKEV1
     ,YG
1001 FORGY=1TO20:NEXTGY,YG:POKE54278,0:
     POKEW1,0:POKEV1,15
1010 REM
1020 REM
```

```
2000 IFA(I)=18680RA(I)=18730RA(I)=1878
     ORA(I)=18900RA(I)=18950RA(I)=1900
     THEN2500
2010 IFA(I)=18840RA(I)=18830RA(I)=1885
     ORA(I)=18860RA(I)=18440RA(I)=1845
     THEN2500
2020 IFA(I)>1984THEN2505
2030 GOTO70
2500 H=H+1:IFH=7THENPRINT"◆ALL BASES
     DESTROYED"
2501 IFH=7THENSS=SS+S*10:PRINT:PRINT
     "YOU SCORED'"SS*10"'":END
2505 PRINT"◆"
2506 IFH<0THENH=0
2507 IFD<0THEND=0
2510 A(1)=1024:A(2)=1034:A(3)=1044:A(4)
     =1054:A(5)=1060
2515 FORT=1TO100:LL=INT(RND(1)*1000):
     POKESC+LL,46:POKECL+LL,1:NEXT
2520 FORI=1904TO1943:POKEI,160:POKEI+CO
     ,2:NEXT
2530 PRINT"◆▓▓▓▓▓▓▓▓▓▓▓▓▓▓▓▓▓▓▓▓◣
     ◪ ▮   ◪ ▮    ◪ ▮    ◪   ◼◻◻◼◼  ▮"
2531 PRINTSPC(26)"◥▲ ▮    ◪ ▮    ◪ ▮"
2550 SS=SS+S:S=0:X=10:Y=19:GOTO60

READY.


0 REM**NUCLEAR ATTACK** KEYBOARD VERSION
1 V1=54296:A1=54277:W1=54276:H1=54273:
  H2=54272
5 POKE6 0,255
```

```
10 POKE53281,0:PRINT"█▓██SKILL LEVEL
   (1-6)"
11 PRINT:PRINT"██▒LEVEL ▙6=█'▙PRO█'"
12 PRINT:PRINT"LEVEL ▙1=█'▙AMATEUR█'"
20 INPUTL
21 IFL=1THEND=20
22 IFL=2THEND=6
23 IFL=3THEND=5
24 IFL=4THEND=3
25 IFL=5THEND=2
26 IFL=6THEND=0:L=5
29 PRINT"▌"
30 IFL<1ORL>6THEN10
40 X=20:Y=19:SC=1024:CO=54272:CL=55296
50 A(1)=1024:A(2)=1034:A(3)=1044:A(4)=
   1054:A(5)=1060
55 FORT=1TO100:LL=INT(RND(1)*1000):POKE
   SC+LL,46:POKECL+LL,1:NEXT
56 FORI=1904TO1943:POKEI,160:POKEI+CO,
   2:NEXT
57 PRINT"█████████████████████████▲    █ █
         █ █    █ █    █  ███▙ █"
58 PRINTSPC(26)"█▲ █    █ █    █ █"
60 FORI=1TOL:IFA(I)=0THEN130
61 IFI=6THEN60
62 A(I)=A(I)+INT(RND(1)*3+39)
63 IFA(I)>1806THEN1000
64 IFA(I)>1904THEN1000
70 POKEA(I),102:POKEA(I)+CO,I
71 FORU=1TOD*10:NEXT
75 POKESC+X+40*Y,32
76 PRINT"████SCORE:"SS*10;" HITS:"H
80 GETA$:IFA$="I"THENY=Y-2
90 IFA$="J"THENX=X-2
100 IFA$="K"THENX=X+2
```

36

```
110  IFA$="M"THENY=Y+2
111  IFA$=" "THEN300
120  POKESC+X+40*Y,91:POKECL+X+40*Y,4
130  NEXT:GOTO60
300  POKEV1,15:POKEA1,9:FORM=128TO255STEP
     5:POKEW1,17:POKEH1,M:POKEH2,M:POKEW1
     ,0
301  NEXT
310  FORM1=1TO15:NEXTM1
400  P=SC+X+40*Y
401  POKEP-40,79:POKEP-39,80:POKEP+40,76
     :POKEP+41,122:POKEP,101:POKEP+1,103
402  P=CL+X+40*Y
403  POKEP-40,1:POKEP-39,1:POKEP+40,1:
     POKEP+41,1:POKEP,1:POKEP+1,1
404  FORU1=1TO80:NEXT:P=SC+X+40*Y
405  POKEP-40,32:POKEP-39,32:POKEP+40,32:
     POKEP+41,32:POKEP,32:POKEP+1,32
410  POKEP-41,85:POKEP-40,64:POKEP-39,73:
     POKEP-1,93:POKEP+1,93:POKEP+39,74:
     POKEP+ 40,64
411  P=CL+X+40*Y
413  POKEP-41,1:POKEP-40,1:POKEP-39,1:
     POKEP-1,1:POKEP+1,1:POKEP+21,1:POKE
     P+40,1
420  POKEP+41,1
421  P=SC+X+40*Y
430  FORZ=1TOL:O=A(Z)
440  IFO=P-41ORO=P-400RO=P-390RO=P-10RO=
     P+10RO=P+390RO=P+400RO=P+41THENA(Z)
     S=S:O=+1
441  IFS=LTHENH=H-1:SS=SS+INT(RND(1)*200)
     +1:D=D-1:GOTO2505
450  NEXT
451  POKEP-41,32:POKEP-40,32:POKEP-39,32
     :POKEP-1,32:POKEP+1,32:POKEP+39,32:
      POKEP+ 40,32
```

```
452 POKEP+41,32
500 GOTO60
1000 POKE54278,240:POKEH1,40:POKEH2,200
     :POKEW1,129:FORYG=15TO0STEP-1:POKE
     V1,YG
1001 FORGY=1TO20:NEXTGY,YG:POKE54278,0:
     POKEW1,0:POKEV1,15
1010 REM
1020 REM
2000 IFA(I)=1868ORA(I)=1873ORA(I)=1878O
     RA(I)=1890ORA(I)=1895ORA(I)=1900
     THEN2500
2010 IFA(I)=1884ORA(I)=1883ORA(I)=1885
     ORA(I)=1886ORA(I)=1844ORA(I)=1845
     THEN2500
2020 IFA(I)>1984THEN2505
2030 GOTO70
2500 H=H+1:IFH=7THENPRINT"    ALL BASES
     DESTROYED"
2501 IFH=7THENSS=SS+S*10:PRINT:PRINT
     "YOU SCORED'"SS*10"'":END
2505 PRINT"  "
2506 IFH<0THENH=0
2507 IFD<0THEND=0
2510 A(1)=1024:A(2)=1034:A(3)=1044:A(4)
     =1054:A(5)=1060
2515 FORT=1TO100:LL=INT(RND(1)*1000):
     POKESC+LL,46:POKECL+LL,1:NEXT
2520 FORI=1904TO1943:POKEI,160:POKEI
     +CO,2:NEXT
2530 PRINT"
     "
2531 PRINTSPC(26)"        "
2550 SS=SS+S:S=0:X=10:Y=19:GOTO60

READY.
```

MANOEUVRE

Avoid the oncoming car in the maze in this challenging game.

You move your car in and out of the maze, gaining points as you do so by driving over the dots. You can only move onto another track if you turn at the beginning of an entrance.

In the keyboard version, using the following control keys:
"I" moves you up
"J" moves you left
"K" moves you right
"M" moves you down

```
0 REM**MANOEUVRE** JOYSTICK VERSION
1 POKE2040,192:FORX=192TO195:FORY=0TO62:
  READA:POKEX*64+Y,A:NEXTY,X
5 POKE650,255:W1=54276
6 POKE54296,15:POKE54284,9:POKE54285,240
  :POKE54280,12:POKE54283,17
10 PRINT"◻":POKE53281,0
100 PRINT"◣ ┌─────────────────┐ "
110 PRINT"|................... | "
120 PRINT"|. ┌────    ────┐ . | "
130 PRINT"|. |...............|. | "
140 PRINT"|. |. ┌───    ───┐. |. | "
150 PRINT"|. |. |...........|. |. | "
160 PRINT"|. |. |. ┌──    ──┐. |. |. | ":PRINT"
           |  |  |  |        |  |  |  | "
170 PRINT"|. . . . ┌───┐. . . . | "
```

```
171 PRINT"|. . . .|      |. . . .|
    ":PRINT"|. . . .|      |. . . .|"
180 PRINT"|. . . .└────┘. . . .|"
190 PRINT"|.|.|.|........|.|.|.|
    ":PRINT"|.|.|.└──   ──┘.|.|.|"
200 PRINT"|.|.|...........|.|.|
    ":PRINT"|.|.└──   ──┘.|.|"
210 PRINT"|.|...............|.|"
211 PRINT"|.└──   ──┘.|
    ":PRINT"|.................|"
220 PRINT"└────────────────┘"
221 V=53248:POKEV+21,1:POKEV+39,1:POKEV,
    100:POKEV+1,119
230 S=0:X=1084:CO=54272:E=1:A=1745:W=40:
    R=46
240 POKEX,81:POKEX+CO,1
244 GOSUB5000
247 POKEX,32:GOSUB1000
250 X=X-E
251 IFX=ATHENPOKEX,42:POKEX+CO,2:PRINT
    "▒YOU CRASHED":GOTO9000
255 IFPEEK(X)=46THENS=S+1:POKE54277,9:
    POKEW1,17:POKE54273,17:POKE54272,37:
    POKEW1 ,0
256 IFS=178ORS=177ORS=179THENPRINT
    "MISSION COMPLETE":END
260 IFX=1065THENE=-40
270 IFX=1745THENE=-1
280 IFX=1764THENE=40
290 IFX=1162THENE=1
300 IFX=1682THENE=40
320 IFX=1147THENE=-40
330 IFX=1667THENE=-1
340 IFX=1229THENE=-40
350 IFX=1589THENE=-1
```

41

```
360  IFX=1600THENE=40
370  IFX=1240THENE=1
380  IFX=1311THENE=-40
390  IFX=1511THENE=-1
410  IFX=1318THENE=1
420  IFX=1084THENE=1
430  IFX=1518THENE=40
440  IFE=40THENPOKE2040,193
450  IFE=-40THENPOKE2040,194
460  IFE=1THENPOKE2040,192
470  IFE=-1THENPOKE2040,195
600  GOTO240
1000  JV=PEEK(56320):JV=15-(JVAND15)
1001  IFX=10760RX=13450RX=17540RX=14840RX
     =11560RX=13470RX=16730RX=1482THEN1009
1002  IFX=13490RX=12350RX=15930RX=14800RX
     =13160RX=1524THEN1009
1003  RETURN
1009  IFJV=1ANDX(>1076THENX=X-80
1010  IFJV=4ANDX(>1345THENX=X-2
1020  IFJV=8ANDX(>1484THENX=X+2
1030  IFJV=2ANDX(>1754THENX=X+80
1031  IFX<1024THENX=X+80
1032  IFX>1784THENX=X-80
1040  RETURN
5000  POKEA,90:POKEA+CO,5
5005  FORT=1TO10:NEXT
5006  GOSUB6000
5010  A=A-W
5012  IFPEEK(A)=93THENPOKEA,93:POKEA+CO,3
     :A=A+W
5020  P=PEEK(A):IFP=46THENR=46
5030  IFP=32THENR=32
5050  IFA=1065THENW=-1
5060  IFA=1745THENW=40
```

```
5070  IFA=1764THENW=1
5080  IFA=1162THENW=-40
5090  IFA=1632THENW=1
5120  IFA=1147THENW=-1
5140  IFA=1667THENW=40
5160  IFA=1229THENW=-1
5170  IFA=1589THENW=40
5180  IFA=1600THENW=1
5190  IFA=1240THENW=-40
5200  IFA=1311THENW=-1
5210  IFA=1511THENW=40
5230  IFA=1318THENW=-40
5240  IFA=1084THENW=-40
5250  IFA=1518THENW=1
5500  RETURN
6000  IFA=1076ORA=1345ORA=1754ORA=1484ORA
      =1156ORA=1347ORA=1673ORA=1482THEN6050
6010  IFA=1349ORA=1235ORA=1593ORA=1480ORA
      =1316ORA=1524THEN6050
6019  POKEA,R
6020  RETURN
6050  L=INT(RND(1)*5)+1
6051  POKEA,R
6052  IFA=1345THENA=A+2:RETURN
6053  IFA=1482ORA=1442ORA=1402THENA=A-2
      :RETURN
6054  IFA=1754THENA=A-80:RETURN
6055  IFA=1075THENX=X+80:RETURN
6056  IFA=1316THENA=A-80:RETURN
6060  IFL=1THENA=A+80
6070  IFL=2THENA=A-80
6080  IFL=3THENA=A-2
6090  IFL=4THENA=A+2
6101  IFA>1784THENA=A-80
6102  IFA<1024THENA=A+80
6120  RETURN
```

```
9000 REM*****END****
9001 IFE=40ORE=-40THENPOKE2041,193:
     POKE2040,194
9002 IFE=10RE=-1THENPOKE2041,195:
     POKE2040,192
9003 POKEV+21,3:POKEV+40,5:POKEV,112:
     POKEV+2,87:POKEV+3,119
9005 V1=54296:POKE54278,240
9010 POKE54284,0:POKE54285,0:POKE54280,0:
     POKE54283,0
9020 POKE54277,9:POKE54273,40:POKE54272,
     200:FORYG=15TO0STEP-1:POKEW1,129:
     POKEV1,YG
9030 FORGY=1TO20:NEXTGY:POKEW1,0:NEXT
9040 POKE54272,0:POKE54273,0:POKE54277,0
     :POKE54296,0:POKE54278,0
9050 PRINT"▤"SPC(25)"▨▨":PRINTSPC(25)"▨▨
     ▨YOUR RATING▨ "
9060 PRINTSPC(25)"▨▨                "
9070 IFS<40THENA$="BACK SEAT DRIVER"
9080 IFS>39ANDS<100THENA$="JUST A PASS!"
9090 IFS>99ANDS<140THENA$="NICE EFFORT"
9100 IFS>139THENA$="'AS GOOD AS A PRO'"
9110 PRINT:PRINT:PRINTSPC(23)"▟ "A$
9120 B$="▨▨▨▨▨▨▨▨▨▨▨▨▨▨▨▨▨▨"
9130 PRINTB$SPC(25)"▟ANOTHER GO?"
9140 GETA$
9150 PRINTB$SPC(25)"            "
9160 IFA$<>"Y"ANDA$<>"N"THEN9120
9170 IFA$="Y"THENGOTO5
9180 PRINT"▢":POKEV+21,0:END
9200 REM*********SPRITE DATA*********
9210 DATA0,0,0,0,0,126,0,0,126,63,0,126,
     63,0,126,63,0,126,63,0,24,12,63,252
9220 DATA31,239,255,117,207,254,223,207,
```

44

```
      254,223,207,254,117,207,254,31,239,255
9230 DATA12,63,252,63,0,24,63,0,126,63,
     0,126,63,0,126,0,0,126,0,0,126
9240 DATA0,56,0,60,238,120,60,254,120,
     63,255,248,63,125,248,61,255,120,
     61,125,12 0
9250 DATA1,255,0,1,255,0,1,255,0,3,1,128
     ,2,0,128,3,255,128,3,255,128,251,
     255,190
9260 DATA251,255,190,255,255,190,255,255
     ,254,255,255,254,251,255,190,249,255
     ,62
9270 DATA1,1,0
9280 DATA1,2,0,251,255,124,251,255,124,,
     255,255,252,255,255,252,251,255,124
9290 DATA251,255,124,3,255,0,2,1,0,3,207
     ,0,1,254,0,1,254,0,1,254,0,1,182,0
9300 DATA60,252,240,60,180,240,63,255,
     240,63,255,240,60,204,240,60,120,
     240,0,0,0
9310 DATA127,128,0,127,128,0,127,129,254
     ,127,129,254,127,129,254,28,1,254
9320 DATA63,224,48,255,191,240,127,158,
     190,127,159,255,127,159,253,127,
     159,255
9330 DATA127,158,190,255,191,240,63,224,
     48,28,1,254,127,1,254,127,1,254,
     127,1,25 4
9340 DATA127,0,0,127,0,0

READY.
```

45

```
0 REM**MANOEUVRE**    KEYBOARD VERSION
1 POKE2040,192:FORX=192TO195:FORY=0TO62
  :READA:POKEX*64+Y,A:NEXTY,X
5 POKE650,255:W1=54276
6 POKE54296,15:POKE54284,9:POKE54285,
  240:POKE54280,12:POKE54283,17
10 PRINT"":POKE53281,0
100 PRINT" ┌─────────────────────┐ "
110 PRINT"|.....................|"
120 PRINT"|.┌────────  ────────┐.|"
130 PRINT"|.|.................|.|"
140 PRINT"|.|.┌──────  ──────┐.|.|"
150 PRINT"|.|.|.............|.|.|"
160 PRINT"|.|.|.┌────    ────┐.|.|.|"
   :PRINT"|  |  |  |        |  |  |  |"
170 PRINT"|.  .  .┌──────┐.  .  .|"
171 PRINT"|.  .  .|      |.  .  .|"
   :PRINT"|.  .  .|      |.  .  .|"
180 PRINT"|.  .  .└──────┘.  .  .|"
190 PRINT"|.|.|.|.........|.|.|.|"
   :PRINT"|.|.|.└──    ──┘.|.|.|"
200 PRINT"|.|.|.............|.|.|"
   :PRINT"|.|.└────    ────┘.|.|"
210 PRINT"|.|.................|.|"
211 PRINT"|.└────────  ────────┘.|"
   :PRINT"|.....................|"
220 PRINT" └─────────────────────┘ "
221 V=53248:POKEV+21,1:POKEV+39,1:POKE
    V,100:POKEV+1,119
230 S=0:X=1084:CO=54272:E=1:A=1745:
    W=40:R=46
240 POKEX,81:POKEX+CO,1
244 GOSUB5000
247 POKEX,32:GOSUB1000
250 X=X-E
```

```
251 IFX=ATHENPOKEX,42:POKEX+CO,2:PRINT
    "⬛YOU CRASHED":GOTO9000
255 IFPEEK(X)=46THENS=S+1:POKE54277,9:
    POKEW1,17:POKE54273,17:POKE54272,37
    :POKEW1,0
256 IFS=1780RS=1770RS=179THENPRINT
    "MISSION COMPLETE":END
260 IFX=1065THENE=-40
270 IFX=1745THENE=-1
280 IFX=1764THENE=40
290 IFX=1162THENE=1
300 IFX=1682THENE=40
320 IFX=1147THENE=-40
330 IFX=1667THENE=-1
340 IFX=1229THENE=-40
350 IFX=1589THENE=-1
360 IFX=1600THENE=40
370 IFX=1240THENE=1
380 IFX=1311THENE=-40
390 IFX=1511THENE=-1
410 IFX=1318THENE=1
420 IFX=1084THENE=1
430 IFX=1518THENE=40
440 IFE=40THENPOKE2040,193
450 IFE=-40THENPOKE2040,194
460 IFE=1THENPOKE2040,192
470 IFE=-1THENPOKE2040,195
600 GOTO240
1000 GETA$
1001 IFX=10760RX=13450RX=17540RX=14840R
     X=11560RX=13470RX=16730RX=1482THEN
     1009
1002 IFX=13490RX=12350RX=15930RX=14800R
     X=13160RX=1524THEN1009
1003 RETURN
```

47

```
1009  IFA$="I"ANDX<>1076THENX=X-80
1010  IFA$="J"ANDX<>1345THENX=X-2
1020  IFA$="K"ANDX<>1484THENX=X+2
1030  IFA$="M"ANDX<>1754THENX=X+80
1031  IFX<1024THENX=X+80
1032  IFX>1784THENX=X-80
1040  RETURN
5000  POKEA,90:POKEA+CO,5
5005  FORT=1TO10:NEXT
5006  GOSUB6000
5010  A=A-W
5012  IFPEEK(A)=93THENPOKEA,93:POKEA+CO,
      3:A=A+W
5020  P=PEEK(A):IFP=46THENR=46
5030  IFP=32THENR=32
5050  IFA=1065THENW=-1
5060  IFA=1745THENW=40
5070  IFA=1764THENW=1
5080  IFA=1162THENW=-40
5090  IFA=1682THENW=1
5120  IFA=1147THENW=-1
5140  IFA=1667THENW=40
5160  IFA=1229THENW=-1
5170  IFA=1589THENW=40
5180  IFA=1600THENW=1
5190  IFA=1240THENW=-40
5200  IFA=1311THENW=-1
5210  IFA=1511THENW=40
5230  IFA=1318THENW=-40
5240  IFA=1084THENW=-40
5250  IFA=1518THENW=1
5500  RETURN
6000  IFA=1076ORA=1345ORA=1754ORA=1484OR
      A=1156ORA=1347ORA=1673ORA=1482THEN
      6050
6010  IFA=1349ORA=1235ORA=1593ORA=1480OR
```

```
       A=1316ORA=1524THEN6050
6019 POKEA,R
6020 RETURN
6050 L=INT(RND(1)*5)+1
6051 POKEA,R
6052 IFA=1345THENA=A+2:RETURN
6053 IFA=1482ORA=1442ORA=1402THENA=A-2:
     RETURN
6054 IFA=1754THENA=A-80:RETURN
6055 IFA=1075THENX=X+80:RETURN
6056 IFA=1316THENA=A-80:RETURN
6060 IFL=1THENA=A+80
6070 IFL=2THENA=A-80
6080 IFL=3THENA=A-2
6090 IFL=4THENA=A+2
6101 IFA>1784THENA=A-80
6102 IFA<1024THENA=A+80
6120 RETURN
9000 REM*****END****
9001 IFE=40ORE=-40THENPOKE2041,193:POKE
     2040,194
9002 IFE=1ORE=-1THENPOKE2041,195:POKE
     2040,192
9003 POKEV+21,3:POKEV+40,5:POKEV,112:
     POKEV+2,87:POKEV+3,119
9005 V1=54296:POKE54278,240
9010 POKE54284,0:POKE54285,0:POKE54280,
     0:POKE54283,0
9020 POKE54277,9:POKE54273,40:POKE54272
     ,200:FORYG=15TO0STEP-1:POKEW1,129:
     POKEV1,YG
9030 FORGY=1TO20:NEXTGY:POKEW1,0:NEXT
9040 POKE54272,0:POKE54273,0:POKE54277,0
     :POKE54296,0:POKE54278,0
9050 PRINT"█"SPC(25)"▓█             ":
     PRINTSPC(25)"▓█ █YOUR RATING█ "
```

```
9060 PRINTSPC(25)"█            "
9070 IFS<40THENA$="BACK SEAT DRIVER"
9080 IFS>39ANDS<100THENA$="JUST A PASS!"
9090 IFS>99ANDS<140THENA$="NICE EFFORT"
9100 IFS>139THENA$="'AS GOOD AS A PRO'"
9110 PRINT:PRINT:PRINTSPC(23)"█ "A$
9120 B$="█████████████████████████"
9130 PRINTB$SPC(25)"█ANOTHER GO?"
9140 GETA$
9150 PRINTB$SPC(25)"             "
9160 IFA$<>"Y"ANDA$<>"N"THEN9120
9170 IFA$="Y"THENGOTO5
9180 PRINT"█":POKEV+21,0:END
9200 REM*********SPRITE DATA*********
9210 DATA0,0,0,0,0,126,0,0,126,63,0,126
     ,63,0,126,63,0,126,63,0,24,12,63,
     252
9220 DATA31,239,255,117,207,254,223,207,
     254,223,207,254,117,207,254,31,
     239,255
9230 DATA12,63,252,63,0,24,63,0,126,63,
     0,126,63,0,126,0,0,126,0,0,126
9240 DATA0,56,0,60,238,120,60,254,120,
     63,255,248,63,125,248,61,255,120,
     61,125,120
9250 DATA1,255,0,1,255,0,1,255,0,3,1,
     128,2,0,128,3,255,128,3,255,128,251
     ,255,190
9260 DATA251,255,190,255,255,190,255,
     255,254,255,255,254,251,255,190,249
     ,255,62
9270 DATA1,1,0
9280 DATA1,2,0,251,255,124,251,255,124,
     255,255,252,255,255,252,251,255,124
9290 DATA251,255,124,3,255,0,2,1,0,3,207
     ,0,1,254,0,1,254,0,1,254,0,1,182,0
```

```
9300 DATA60,252,240,60,180,240,63,255,
     240,63,255,240,60,204,240,60,120,
     240,0,0,0
9310 DATA127,128,0,127,128,0,127,129,
     254,127,129,254,127,129,254,28,1,254
9320 DATA63,224,48,255,191,240,127,158,
     190,127,159,255,127,159,253,127,159,
     255
9330 DATA127,158,190,255,191,240,63,224,
     48,28,1,254,127,1,254,127,1,254,127
     ,1,254
9340 DATA127,0,0,127,0,0

READY.
```

BARREL JUMPER

A mad lizard has captured your beloved. Can you save the day?

To do so, you'll have to climb ladders and jump over the barrels the lizard throws down at you. Once you've climbed the last ladder, a lever to your left will be raised. This will allow you to jump into the lizard's mouth, and save your lover.

But, be ye warned, oh brave hero! If the lizard sticks his tongue out, and you jump into his mouth, you'll be eaten. If the lever falls back down, you'll have to go back to the top of the ladder to raise it again.

The controls for keyboard players are:
"W" to move up
"X" to move down
"A" to move left
"D" to move right

The space bar allows you to jump. You use the fire button to jump when playing the joystick version.

```
0 REM**BARREL JUMPER** JOYSTICK VERSION
1 POKE2040,195:POKE2041,193:POKE2042,
  194:POKE2043,195:POKE2044,196:POKE
  2047,195
2 V1=54296:A1=54277:W1=54276:H1=54273:
  H2=54272:POKE2045,195:POKE2046,195
```

```
3 FORX=192TO196
4 FORY=0TO62:READA:POKEX*64+Y,A:NEXTY,X
5 V=53248:POKEV+21,255:POKEV+41,7:POKEV
  +2,76:POKEV+3,50
6 POKEV+29,2
10 PRINT"◼":POKE53280,0:POKE53281,0:
   CO=54272
11 POKE1186+CO,6:POKE1185+CO,6:POKE1146
   +CO,S:POKE1147+CO,6
12 PRINT"◼◼◼◼◼◼◼◼◼◼◼"SPC(27)
   "◼B A R R E L":PRINT:PRINTSPC(27)
   "J U M P E R"
20 PRINT"◼       ◼ ◼◼◼◼◼◼◼◼◼◼◼◼◼◼
   JJJ◼◼ |  \◼◼◼◼◼\X\◼◼◼◼\X\◼◼◼\X\"
30 PRINT"◼◼◼◼◼◼◼◼ ┌─◼
   ──◼":PRINT"    ├──┤◼◼◼◼◼├──┤◼◼◼◼◼├──┤";
31 PRINT"◼◼◼◼◼├──┤ "
40 PRINT"◼        ───────────────────────"
45 PRINTSPC(21)"◼├──┤◼◼◼◼◼├──┤◼◼◼◼◼├──┤
   ◼◼◼◼◼├──┤ "
50 PRINT"◼     ──────────────────────────"
55 PRINT"◼◼◼◼◼├──┤◼◼◼◼◼├──┤◼◼◼◼◼├──┤◼◼◼◼◼
   ├──┤ "
60 PRINT"◼       ──────────────────────"
65 PRINTSPC(21)"◼◼◼   ┌◼◼◼◼◼┘"
75 UU=10:II=11:OO=12:PP=13:JJ=14:U(1)=
   150:I(1)=150
80 X=173:Y=190:Q=0:U=100:I=200:T(1)=1:
   T(2)=1:POKEV1,15
90 POKEV+4,X:POKEV+5,Y:POKEV+21,255
91 POKE54277,9:POKE54296,15:POKE54273,17
   :POKE54272,37:POKE54276,17:POKE54276,0
93 PRINT"◼"SPC(24)"◼SCORE:"S
94 L=INT(RND(1)*20)+1:IFL<>1ANDL<>2ANDL
   <>3ANDL<>4ANDL<>5THEN104
```

```
95  IFL=1ANDT(1)<>1THENT(1)=1:GOSUB1000
96  IFL=2ANDT(2)<>1THENT(2)=1:GOSUB1000
97  IFL=3ANDT(3)<>1THENT(3)=1:GOSUB1000
98  IFL=4ANDT(4)<>1THENT(4)=1:GOSUB1000
99  IFL=5ANDT(5)<>1THENT(5)=1:GOSUB1000
104 JV=PEEK(56320):FR=JVAND16:JV=15-
    (JVAND15)
105 IFFR=0THENGOSUB300
106 IFX=53ANDY=71THENPOKE1225,32:POKE
    1226,32:TI$="000000":POKE1185,78:
    POKE1186,126:E=1
107 IFE=1ANDTI$>"000010"THENPOKE1185,32
    :POKE1186,32:POKE1225,99:POKE1226,
    126:E=0
108 IFE=1ANDRND(1)>.7THENPOKE1079,104:
    C=2:PRINT"▧▲        "
109 IFE=1ANDRND(1)>.82THENPOKE1079,32:
    C=1:PRINT"▧▲▧HELP!"
110 IFJV=0THEN143
111 IFJV=4THENX=X-10:IFX<53THENX=53
120 IFJV=8THENX=X+10:IFX>193THENX=193
130 IFJV=1ANDX=53ANDY=190THENY=150
131 IFJV=1ANDX=193ANDY=150THENY=111
132 IFJV=1ANDX=53ANDY=111THENY=71
140 IFJV=2ANDX=53ANDY=150THENY=190
141 IFJV=2ANDX=193ANDY=111THENY=150
142 IFJV=2ANDX=53ANDY=71THENY=1.11
143 IFU>X-15ANDU<X+12ANDU(1)=YTHEN2000
144 IFI>X-15ANDI<X+12ANDI(1)=YTHEN2000
145 IFO>X-15ANDO<X+12ANDO(1)=YTHEN2000
146 IFP>X-15ANDP<X+12ANDP(1)=YTHEN2000
147 IFJ>X-15ANDJ<X+12ANDJ(1)=YTHEN2000
148 POKEV+4,X:POKEV+5,Y
155 GOSUB3200
156 GOTO90
300 IFC=1ANDX=133ANDY=71ANDE=1THEN1500
```

55

```
301  IFC=2ANDX=133ANDY=71THEN2000
302  Y=Y-15:POKEV+21,255:POKEV+8,X:POKE
     V+9,Y:POKEV+4,0:POKEV+5,0
303  XX=1:FORR=1TO6:GOSUB3200:NEXT
304  Y=Y+15:POKEV+8,0:POKEV+9,0:POKEV+4,X
     :POKEV+5,Y
306  XX=0:RETURN
1000 L=INT(RND(1)*100)+100
1003 POKEV+2,L:POKEV+3,50:FORTT=1TO200:
     NEXT:POKEV+39,1
1004 POKE2041,192:FORTT=1TO400:NEXT
1005 POKE2041,193
1010 FORR=50TO70:POKEV,L:POKEV+1,R:NEXT
1020 IFU<=0THENUU=10:U(1)=R:U=L:GOTO1070
1030 IFI<=0THENII=11:I(1)=R:I=L:GOTO1070
1040 IFO<=0THENOO=12:O(1)=R:O=L:GOTO1070
1050 IFP<=0THENPP=13:P(1)=R:P=L:GOTO1070
1060 IFJ<=0THENJJ=14:J(1)=R:J=L
1070 POKEV,U:POKEV+1,U(1)
1160 RETURN
1500 X=173:Y=190:POKE1199,32:POKEA1,9:
     PRINT"▨▨▨SAVED!!"
1510 FORT=STOS+INT(RND(1)*500)+200:POKE
     W1,17:POKEH1,17:POKEH2,37:POKEW1,0
1520 PRINT"◆"SPC(24)"◆SCORE:"T:NEXT:S=T:
     :PRINT"◆          ":GOTO90
2000 IFC=2ANDX=133ANDY=71THENPRINT
     "▨▨▨▨▨▨▨▨THE LIZARD HAD HIS TONGUE
     OUT.BURP!"
2001 CLR:V1=54296:A1=54277:W1=54276:H1=
     54273:H2=54272:POKEV1,15:POKEA1,9
2010 FORA=255TO0STEP-3:POKEW1,17:POKE
     H1,A:POKEH2,A:POKEW1,0
2020 FORR=1TO8:NEXTR,A
2040 END
```

56

```
3200 U=U-UU:I=I-II:O=O-OO:P=P-PP:J=J-JJ
3201 POKE54277,9:POKE54296,15:POKE54273,
     17:POKE54272,37:POKE54276,17
3202 FORYG=1TO5:NEXT:POKE54276,0
3210 IFU<1THENU=0
3220 IFI<1THENI=0
3230 IFO<1THENO=0
3300 IFP<1THENP=0
3400 IFJ<1THENJ=0
3500 POKEV,U:POKEV+6,I:POKEV+10,O:POKE
     V+12,P:POKEV+14,J
3600 POKEV+1,U(1):POKEV+7,I(1):POKEV+11
     ,O(1):POKEV+13,P(1):POKEV+15,J(1)
3700 POKEV+39,1:POKEV+42,1:POKEV+44,1:
     POKEV+45,1:POKEV+46,1
3800 IFU<29ANDU(1)=150THENU(1)=190:UU=-10
3900 IFI<29ANDI(1)=150THENI(1)=190:II=-11
4000 IFO<29ANDO(1)=150THENO(1)=190:OO=-12
4100 IFP<29ANDP(1)=150THENP(1)=190:PP=-13
4200 IFJ<29ANDJ(1)=150THENJ(1)=190:JJ=-14
4300 IFU<29ANDU(1)=71THENU(1)=111:UU=-10
4400 IFI<29ANDI(1)=71THENI(1)=111:II=-11
4500 IFO<29ANDO(1)=71THENO(1)=111:OO=-12
4600 IFP<29ANDP(1)=71THENP(1)=111:PP=-13
4601 IFXX=1THEN4700
4610 JV=PEEK(56320):FR=JVAND16:JV=15-
     (JVAND15)
4630 IFX=53ANDY=71THENPOKE1225,32:POKE
     1226,32:TI$="000000":POKE1185,78:
     POKE1186,1
4640 IFE=1ANDTI$>"000010"THENPOKE1185,
     32:POKE1186,32:POKE1225,99:POKE
     1226,126:E=0
4650 IFE=1ANDRND(1)>.7THENPOKE1079,104:
     C=2:PRINT"▧▲        "
```

57

```
4660  IFE=1ANDRND(1)>.82THENPOKE1079,32:
      C=1:PRINT"▧▤▥HELP!"
4661  IFJV=0THEN4670
4662  IFJV=4THENX=X-10:IFX<53THENX=53
4663  IFJV=8THENX=X+10:IFX>193THENX=193
4664  IFJV=1ANDX=53ANDY=190THENY=150
4665  IFJV=1ANDX=193ANDY=150THENY=111
4666  IFJV=1ANDX=53ANDY=111THENY=71
4667  IFJV=2ANDX=53ANDY=150THENY=190
4668  IFJV=2ANDX=193ANDY=111THENY=150
4669  IFJV=2ANDX=53ANDY=71THENY=111
4670  IFU>X-15ANDU<X+12ANDU(1)=YTHEN2000
4671  IFI>X-15ANDI<X+12ANDI(1)=YTHEN2000
4672  IFO>X-15ANDO<X+12ANDO(1)=YTHEN2000
4673  IFP>X-15ANDP<X+12ANDP(1)=YTHEN2000
4674  IFJ>X-15ANDJ<X+12ANDJ(1)=YTHEN2000
4699  POKEV+4,X:POKEV+5,Y
4700  IFJ<29ANDJ(1)=71THENJ(1)=111:JJ=-14
4800 IFU>211ANDU(1)=111THENU(1)=150:UU=10
4900 IFI>211ANDI(1)=111THENI(1)=150:II=11
4910 IFO>211ANDO(1)=111THENO(1)=150:OO=12
4920 IFP>211ANDP(1)=111THENP(1)=150:PP=13
4930 IFJ>211ANDJ(1)=111THENJ(1)=150:JJ=14
4940 IFU>190ANDU(1)=190THENPOKEV+1,211:
     POKEV,195:U(1)=0:U=0:UU=0:T(1)=0:
     GOSUB5009
4950  IFI>190ANDI(1)=190THENPOKEV+7,211
     :POKEV+6,195:I(1)=0:I=0:II=0:T(2)
     =0:GOSUB5009
4960  IFO>190ANDO(1)=190THENPOKEV+11,211
     :POKEV+10,195:O(1)=0:O=0:OO=0:T(3)
     =0:GOSUB5009
4970  IFP>190ANDP(1)=190THENPOKEV+13,211
     :POKEV+12,195:P=0:PP=0:T(4)=0:
     GOSUB5003
```

```
4980  IF J>190ANDJ(1)=190THENPOKEV+15,211
      :POKEV+14,195:J=0:JJ=0:T(5)=0:
      GOSUB5004
4990  RETURN
5000  POKEA1,9:POKEV1,15:POKEW1,17:POKE
      H1,17:POKEH2,37
5003  P(1)=0:GOTO5009
5004  J(1)=0
5009  S=S+10
5010  POKEA1,9:POKEV1,15:POKEW1,17:POKE
      H1,17:POKEH2,37
5020  POKEW1,0:RETURN
6000  DATA1,248,0,2,4,0,2,148,0,2,4,0,1,
      104,0,126,151,240,128,96,8,128,0,8
6010  DATA136,0,136,136,32,136,143,119,
      136,128,248,8,128,248,8,127,119,240
6020  DATA17,36,64,17,4,64,17,4,64,17,4,
      64,31,7,192,31,7,192,31,7,192
6030  DATA7,126,248,13,255,136,16,126,4,
      35,60,226,38,66,50,36,165,18
6040  DATA39,129,242,32,153,2,32,66,2,31,
      60,252,1,0,128,3,0,224
6050  DATA2,0,32,6,0,48,4,0,16,6,0,48,3,
      156,224,0,148,128,0,247,128
6060  DATA0,247,128,0,247,128
6070  DATA0,126,0,0,225,0,0,225,0,0,129,
      0,0,126,0,7,255,192,15,129,224,31,
      255,240
6075  DATA62,129,112,126,255,112,126,255,
      112,124,129,224
6080  DATA112,255,192,96,129,0,0,255,0,1,
      255,128,3,255,192,7,227,224,15,193,
      240
6090  DATA15,131,240,31,135,240,0,0,0
6100  DATA0,0,0,0,0,0,0,0,0,0,0,0,0,0,0,
      0,0,0,0,0,0,0,0,0,0,0,0,0,127,0
```

```
6110 DATA0,255,128,1,255,192,3,255,224,
     7,255,240,7,255,240,7,255,240,7,255
     ,240
6120 DATA3,255,224,1,255,192,0,255,128,
     0,127,0
6130 DATA48,63,3,56,82,135,60,76,143,62,
     63,30,31,255,252,15,128,120,7,255,
     240
6140 DATA1,128,96,0,255,192,0,128,64,0,
     255,192,0,128,64,0,255,192,0,255,
     192
6150 DATA1,255,224,3,255,240,7,192,248,
     15,128,124,31,0,62,62,0,31,62,0,31
```

READY.

```
0 REM**BARREL JUMPER** KEYBOARD VERSION
1 POKE2040,195:POKE2041,193:POKE2042,194
  :POKE2043,195:POKE2044,196:POKE2047,
  195
2 V1=54296:A1=54277:W1=54276:H1=54273:
  H2=54272:POKE2045,195:POKE2046,195
3 FORX=192TO196
4 FORY=0TO62:READA:POKEX*64+Y,A:NEXTY,X
5 V=53248:POKEV+21,255:POKEV+41,7:POKEV
  +2,76:POKEV+3,50
6 POKEV+29,2
10 PRINT"█":POKE53280,0:POKE53281,0:CO
   =54272
11 POKE1186+CO,6:POKE1185+CO,6:POKE1146
   +CO,6:POKE1147+CO,6
12 PRINT"███████████████"SPC(27)
   "█B A R R E L":PRINT:PRINTSPC(27)
```

60

```
   "J U M P E R"
20 PRINT"█        █. ░█████████████
   JJJ█ | \███▔\XX\███X\███XX\"
30 PRINT"█████████ ▔▀▚_____
   ──█":PRINT"     ├──┤█████├──┤ ▒████
   ├──┤";
31 PRINT"█████├──┤ "
40 PRINT"▚     ─────────────────────────"
45 PRINTSPC(21)"█├──┤█████├──┤█████├──┤
   █████├──┤ "
50 PRINT"▚   ─────────────────────────"
55 PRINT"█████├──┤█████├──┤█████├──┤
   █████├──┤ "
60 PRINT"▚     ──────────────────"
65 PRINTSPC(21)"██ ▔█████▁"
75 UU=10:II=11:OO=12:PP=13:JJ=14:U(1)=
   150:I(1)=150
80 X=173:Y=190:Q=0:U=100:I=200:T(1)=1:
   T(2)=1:POKEV1,15
90 POKEV+4,X:POKEV+5,Y:POKEV+21,255
91 POKE54277,9:POKE54296,15:POKE54273,
   17:POKE54272,37:POKE54276,17:POKE
   54276,0
93 PRINT"█"SPC(24)"█SCORE:"S
94 L=INT(RND(1)*20)+1:IFL<>1ANDL<>2AND
   L<>3ANDL<>4ANDL<>5THEN104
95 IFL=1ANDT(1)<>1THENT(1)=1:GOSUB1000
96 IFL=2ANDT(2)<>1THENT(2)=1:GOSUB1000
97 IFL=3ANDT(3)<>1THENT(3)=1:GOSUB1000
98 IFL=4ANDT(4)<>1THENT(4)=1:GOSUB1000
98 IFL=5ANDT(5)<>1THENT(5)=1:GOSUB1000
104 K=PEEK(197)
105 IFK=60THENGOSUB300
106 IFX=53ANDY=71THENPOKE1225,32:POKE
    1226,32:TI$="000000":POKE1185,78:
```

61

```
    POKE1186,126:E=1
107 IFE=1ANDTI$>"000010"THENPOKE1185,32
    :POKE1186,32:POKE1225,99:POKE1226,
    126:E=0
108 IFE=1ANDRND(1)>.7THENPOKE1079,104:
    C=2:PRINT"🔺        "
109 IFE=1ANDRND(1)>.82THENPOKE1079,32:
    C=1:PRINT"🔺🔺HELP!"
110 IFK=64THEN143
111 IFK=10THENX=X-10:IFX<53THENX=53
120 IFK=18THENX=X+10:IFX>193THENX=193
130 IFK=9ANDX=53ANDY=190THENY=150
131 IFK=9ANDX=193ANDY=150THENY=111
132 IFK=9ANDX=53ANDY=111THENY=71
140 IFK=23ANDX=53ANDY=150THENY=190
141 IFK=23ANDX=193ANDY=111THENY=150
142 IFK=23ANDX=53ANDY=71THENY=111
143 IFU>X-15ANDU<X+12ANDU(1)=YTHEN2000
144 IFI>X-15ANDI<X+12ANDI(1)=YTHEN2000
145 IFO>X-15ANDO<X+12ANDO(1)=YTHEN2000
146 IFP>X-15ANDP<X+12ANDP(1)=YTHEN2000
147 IFJ>X-15ANDJ<X+12ANDJ(1)=YTHEN2000
148 POKEV+4,X:POKEV+5,Y
155 GOSUB3200
156 GOTO90
300 IFC=1ANDX=133ANDY=71ANDE=1THEN1500
301 IFC=2ANDX=133ANDY=71THEN2000
302 Y=Y-15:POKEV+21,255:POKEV+8,X:POKE
    V+9,Y:POKEV+4,0:POKEV+5,0
303 XX=1:FORR=1TO6:GOSUB3200:NEXT
304 Y=Y+15:POKEV+8,0:POKEV+9,0:POKEV+4,
    X:POKEV+5,Y
306 XX=0:RETURN
1000 L=INT(RND(1)*100)+100
1003 POKEV+2,L:POKEV+3,50:FORTT=1TO200:
     NEXT:POKEV+39,1
```

```
1004  POKE2041,192:FORTT=1TO400:NEXT
1005  POKE2041,193
1010  FORR=50TO70:POKEV,L:POKEV+1,R:NEXT
1020  IFU<=0THENUU=10:U(1)=R:U=L:GOTO1070
1030  IFI<=0THENII=11:I(1)=R:I=L:GOTO1070
1040  IFO<=0THENOO=12:O(1)=R:O=L:GOTO1070
1050  IFP<=0THENPP=13:P(1)=R:P=L:GOTO1070
1060  IFJ<=0THENJJ=14:J(1)=R:J=L
1070  POKEV,U:POKEV+1,U(1)
1160  RETURN
1500  X=173:Y=190:POKE1199,32:POKEA1,9:
      PRINT"████SAVED!!"
1510  FORT=STOS+INT(RND(1)*500)+200:POKE
      W1,17:POKEH1,17:POKEH2,37:POKEW1,0
1520  PRINT"█"SPC(24)"█SCORE:"T:NEXT:S=T:
      :PRINT"█          ":GOTO90
2000  IFC=2ANDX=133ANDY=71THENPRINT
      "████████████THE LIZARD HAD HIS TONGUE
      OUT.BURP!"
2001  CLR:V1=54296:A1=54277:W1=54276:
      H1=54273:H2=54272:POKEV1,15:POKEA1,9
2010  FORA=255TO0STEP-3:POKEW1,17:POKE
      H1,A:POKEH2,A:POKEW1,0
2020  FORR=1TO8:NEXTR,A
2040  END
3200  U=U-UU:I=I-II:O=O-OO:P=P-PP:J=J-JJ
3201  POKE54277,9:POKE54296,15:POKE54273,
      17:POKE54272,37:POKE54276,17
3202  FORYG=1TO5:NEXT:POKE54276,0
3210  IFU<1THENU=0
3220  IFI<1THENI=0
3230  IFO<1THENO=0
3300  IFP<1THENP=0
3400  IFJ<1THENJ=0
3500  POKEV,U:POKEV+6,I:POKEV+10,O:POKE
```

63

```
       V+12,P:POKEV+14,J
 3600  POKEV+1,U(1):POKEV+7,I(1):POKEV+11
       ,O(1):POKEV+13,P(1):POKEV+15,J(1)
 3700  POKEV+39,1:POKEV+42,1:POKEV+44,1:
       POKEV+45,1:POKEV+46,1
 3800 IFU<29ANDU(1)=150THENU(1)=190:UU=-10
 3900 IFI<29ANDI(1)=150THENI(1)=190:II=-11
 4000 IFO<29ANDO(1)=150THENO(1)=190:OO=-12
 4100 IFP<29ANDP(1)=150THENP(1)=190:PP=-13
 4200 IFJ<29ANDJ(1)=150THENJ(1)=190:JJ=-14
 4300  IFU<29ANDU(1)=71THENU(1)=111:UU=-10
 4400  IFI<29ANDI(1)=71THENI(1)=111:II=-11
 4500  IFO<29ANDO(1)=71THENO(1)=111i:OO=-12
 4600  IFP<29ANDP(1)=71THENP(1)=111:PP=-13
 4601  IFXX=1THEN4700
 4610  K=PEEK(197)
 4630  IFX=53ANDY=71THENPOKE1225,32:POKE
       1226,32:TI$="000000":POKE1185,78:
       POKE1186,1
 4640  IFE=1ANDTI$>"000010"THENPOKE1185,
       32:POKE1186,32:POKE1225,99:POKE
       1226,126:E=0
 4650  IFE=1ANDRND(1)>.7THENPOKE1079,104
       :C=2:PRINT"        "
 4660  IFE=1ANDRND(1)>.82THENPOKE1079,32:
       C=1:PRINT"  HELP!"
 4661  IFK=64THEN4670
 4662  IFK=10THENX=X-10:IFX<53THENX=53
 4663  IFK=18THENX=X+10:IFX>193THENX=193
 4664  IFK=9ANDX=53ANDY=190THENY=150
 4665  IFK=9ANDX=193ANDY=150THENY=111
 4666  IFK=9ANDX=53ANDY=111THENY=71
 4667  IFK=23ANDX=53ANDY=150THENY=190
 4668  IFK=23ANDX=193ANDY=111THENY=150
 4669  IFK=23ANDX=53ANDY=71THENY=111
```

64

```
4670   IFU>X-15ANDU<X+12ANDU(1)=YTHEN2000
4671   IFI>X-15ANDI<X+12ANDI(1)=YTHEN2000
4672   IFO>X-15ANDO<X+12ANDO(1)=YTHEN2000
4673   IFP>X-15ANDP<X+12ANDP(1)=YTHEN2000
4674   IFJ>X-15ANDJ<X+12ANDJ(1)=YTHEN2000
4699   POKEV+4,X:POKEV+5,Y
4700   IFJ<29ANDJ(1)=71THENJ(1)=111:JJ=-14
4800 IFU>211ANDU(1)=111THENU(1)=150:UU=10
4900 IFI>211ANDI(1)=111THENI(1)=150:II=11
4910 IFO>211ANDO(1)=111THENO(1)=150:OO=12
4920 IFP>211ANDP(1)=111THENP(1)=150:PP=13
4930 IFJ>211ANDJ(1)=111THENJ(1)=150:JJ=14
4940   IFU>190ANDU(1)=190THENPOKEV+1,211:
       POKEV,195:U(1)=0:U=0:UU=0:T(1)=0:
       GOSUB5009
4950   IFI>190ANDI(1)=190THENPOKEV+7,211:
       POKEV+6,195:I(1)=0:I=0:II=0:T(2)=0:
       GOSUB5009
4960   IFO>190ANDO(1)=190THENPOKEV+11,211
     :POKEV+10,195:O(1)=0:O=0:OO=0:T(3)=0:
       GOSUB5009
4970   IFP>190ANDP(1)=190THENPOKEV+13,211:
       POKEV+12,195:P=0:PP=0:T(4)=0:GOSUB
       5003
4980   IFJ>190ANDJ(1)=190THENPOKEV+15,211
     :POKEV+14,195:J=0:JJ=0:T(5)=0:
       GOSUB5004
4990   RETURN
5000   POKEA1,9:POKEV1,15:POKEW1,17:POKE
       H1,17:POKEH2,37
5003   P(1)=0:GOTO5009
5004   J(1)=0
5009   S=S+10
5010   POKEA1,9:POKEV1,15:POKEW1,17:POKE
       H1,17:POKEH2,37
```

65

```
5020 POKEW1,0:RETURN
6000 DATA1,248,0,2,4,0,2,148,0,2,4,0,1,
     104,0,126,151,240,128,96,8,128,0,8
6010 DATA136,0,136,136,32,136,143,119,
     136,128,248,8,128,248,8,127,119,240
6020 DATA17,36,64,17,4,64,17,4,64,17,4,
     64,31,7,192,31,7,192,31,7,192
6030 DATA7,126,248,13,255,136,16,126,4,
     35,60,226,38,66,50,36,165,18
6040 DATA39,129,242,32,153,2,32,66,2,31,
     60,252,1,0,128,3,0,224
6050 DATA2,0,32,6,0,48,4,0,16,6,0,48,3,
     156,224,0,148,128,0,247,128
6060 DATA0,247,128,0,247,128
6070 DATA0,126,0,0,225,0,0,225,0,0,129,
     0,0,126,0,7,255,192,15,129,224,31,
     255,240
6075 DATA62,129,112,126,255,112,126,255,
     112,124,129,224
6080 DATA112,255,192,96,129,0,0,255,0,1,
     255,128,3,255,192,7,227,224,15,193,240
6090 DATA15,131,240,31,135,240,0,0,0
6100 DATA0,0,0,0,0,0,0,0,0,0,0,0,0,0,0,
     0,0,0,0,0,0,0,0,0,0,0,0,0,127,0
6110 DATA0,255,128,1,255,132,3,255,224,
     7,255,240,7,255,240,7,255,240,7,
     255,240
6120 DATA3,255,224,1,255,192,0,255,128,
     0,127,0
6130 DATA48,63,3,56,82,135,60,76,143,62
     ,63,30,31,255,252,15,128,120,7,255,
     240
6140 DATA1,128,96,0,255,192,0,128,64,0,
     255,192,0,128,64,0,255,192,0,255,192
```

```
6150  DATA1,255,224,3,255,240,7,192,248,
      15,128,124,31,0,62,62,0,31,62,0,31

READY.
```

BULLET HEADS

In this wild west game, you attempt to beat the computer. Move up and down the screen, attempting to avoid Outlaw C-64's bullets.

The "I" key moves you up, the "M" moves you down, and the space bar fires your revolver.

```
0 REM**BULLET HEADS**   JOYSTICK VERSION
1 V1=54296:W1=54276:A1=54277:Q1=54278:H1
  =54273:H2=54272
2 POKEV1,15
3 FORA=1TO39:READS:NEXT
5 POKE2045,197:POKE650,128:DIMS(20)
  ,W(20)
6 POKE2040,192:POKE2041,193:POKE2042,
  194:POKE2043,195:POKE2044,196
7 FORH=192TO197
8 FORY=0TO62:READA:POKEH*64+Y,A:NEXTY,H
9 V=53248:POKEV+23,63:POKEV+29,63
10 POKEV+21,63:POKEV+39,15:POKEV+40,1:
   POKEV+41,1:POKEV+42,15:POKEV+43,15:
   POKEV+44,1
11 POKEV,70:POKEV+1,60:POKEV+4,36:POKE
   V+5,62:POKEV+2,120:POKEV+3,60
12 POKEV+8,200:POKEV+9,60:POKEV+6,250:
   POKEV+7,60
13 POKEV+16,32:POKEV+10,40:POKEV+11,60
18 PRINT"◣":X=30:L=7:SC=1024:CL=55296:K
   =13:B=3
19 RESTORE:GOSUB10000
```

```
20 A$="█ⅢⅢⅢⅢⅢⅢⅢⅢⅢⅢⅢⅢⅢ"
30 C$="█ⅢⅢⅢⅢⅢⅢⅢⅢⅢⅢⅢⅢⅢ"
400 PRINT"███                              "
401 PRINT"███OUTLAW VIC"YY:PRINT"█"SPC
    (27)"█SHERIFF"CC
402 IFOO=1THENPRINT"███"SPC(24)"SHERIFF
    LOADING"
403 IFFF=1THENPRINT"███OUTLAW VIC
    LOADING"
409 PRINTLEFT$(A$,L)
410 PRINTTAB(X)"   "
500 PRINTTAB(X)" ∩ ":PRINTTAB(X-3)"    ∪ "
510 PRINTTAB(X-2)"  ██ ██":PRINTTAB
    (X-1)"  ██ ██ "
512 PRINTTAB(X)"  ██ ██ ":PRINTTAB(X-1)"
    ██▀█ ▀"
519 PRINTTAB(X-2)"          "
520 JV=PEEK(56320):FR=JVAND16:JV=15-
    (JVAND15):IFJV=1THENL=L-1
530 IFJV=2THENL=L+1
540 IFFR=0ANDOO=0THEN999
550 IFL<7THENL=7
560 IFL>14THENL=14
570 IFOO=1THENJ=J+1:IFJ=5THENPP=0:OO=0:J
    =0
580 IFFF=1THENG=G+1:IFG=5THENDD=0:FF=0:G
    =0
600 PRINTLEFT$(A$,K)
610 PRINTTAB(B)"   "
620 PRINTTAB(B)" ∩ ":PRINTTAB(B-3)
    "    ∪    "
630 PRINTTAB(B-2)"  ██ ██":PRINTTAB
    (B-1)"  ██ ██ "
640 PRINTTAB(B)"  ██ ██ ":PRINTTAB(B-1)"
    ██▀█ ▀"
650 PRINTTAB(B-2)"          "
```

```
660  IFRND(1)>.65THENK=K+(K>L)-(K<L)
670  IFRND(1)>.6ANDFF=0THEN1999
680  IFK<7THENK=7
690  IFK>14THENK=14
700  GOTO400
999  PRINTLEFT$(A$,L)
1000 PP=PP+1:IFPP=6THENOO=1
1009 PRINTTAB(X)" ⌒ "
1010 PRINTTAB(X)" ⌣ "
1020 PRINTTAB(X-2)"▨▪▮  ▨▪ ▮ "
1030 PRINTTAB(X-1)"▮▨▬▪▬  ▮ "
1040 PRINTTAB(X+1)"▨▮  "
1050 PRINTTAB(X)"▮▬▨ ▮ "
1060 PRINTTAB(X-1)"▮▨▮▮ ▨▮▮▮▪"
1061 POKEW1,129:POKEA1,9:POKEQ1,240:POKE
     H1,40:POKEH2,200:FORYG=15TO0STEP-1
1062 POKEV1,YG:FORGY=1TO10:NEXTGY,YG:
     POKEQ1,0:POKEW1,0
1070 FORR=X-4TO0STEP-1:P=PEEK(SC+R+40*
     (L+2))
1071 IFP=102THENPOKESC+R+40*(L+2),32:
     POKESC+(R+1)+40*(L+2),32:GOTO400
1072 IFP<>32ANDP<>102THEN6000
1080 POKESC+R+40*(L+2),46:POKECL+R+40*
     (L+2),0:POKESC+(R+1)+40*(L+2),32
1090 NEXT:POKESC+(R+1)+40*(L+2),32:
     GOTO400
1999 PRINTLEFT$(C$,K)
2000 DD=DD+1:IFDD=6THENFF=1
2009 PRINTTAB(B)" ⌒  "
2010 PRINTTAB(B)" ⌣   "
2020 PRINTTAB(B)"▨▮ ▮  ▨▮ ▪"
2030 PRINTTAB(B)"▨▮ ▮▮▪▬▨▪"
2040 PRINTTAB(B)"▨▮ ▮   "
2050 PRINTTAB(B)"▮▨ ▮▮▪   "
2060 PRINTTAB(B-1)"▮▬▨ ▨▮ ▨▮▮  "
```

71

```
2065 PRINTTAB(B-1)"          "
2066 POKEW1,129:POKEA1,9:POKEQ1,240:POKE
     H1,40:POKEH2,200:FORYG=15TO0STEP-1
2067 POKEV1,YG:FORGY=1TO10:NEXTGY,YG:
     POKEQ1,0:POKEW1,0
2070 FORR=B+5TO35:D=PEEK(SC+R+40*(K+2))
2071 IFD=102THENPOKESC+R+40*(K+2),32:
     POKESC+(R-1)+40*(K+2),32:GOTO400
2072 IFD<>32ANDD<>102THEN5000
2080 POKESC+R+40*(K+2),46:POKECL+R+40*
     (K+2),0:POKESC+(R-1)+40*(K+2),32
2090 NEXT:POKESC+(R-1)+40*(K+2),32:
     GOTO400
5000 PRINTLEFT$(A$,L)
5010 PRINTTAB(X)"    "
5020 PRINTTAB(X)"   ":PRINTTAB(X-3)
     "         "
5030 PRINTTAB(X-2)"        ":PRINTTAB(X-1)
     "        "
5040 PRINTTAB(X)"     ":PRINTTAB(X-1)"      "
5050 PRINTTAB(X-2)"       "
5060 PRINTLEFT$(C$,K+4)
5070 PRINTTAB(X-3)"O▓  ■ ▆▄▞ "
5075 POKE54278,180
5080 POKEV1,15:POKEA1,9:FORT=1TO19:READS
     :READD:POKEW1,17:POKEH1,S:POKEH2,S
5090 FORTT=1TOD:NEXT:POKEW1,0:NEXT
5095 RESTORE
5100 YY=YY+1:GOTO6120
6000 PRINTLEFT$(A$,K)
6010 PRINTTAB(B)"    "
6020 PRINTTAB(B)"     ":PRINTTAB
     (B-3)"         "
6030 PRINTTAB(B-2)"        ":PRINTTAB
     (B-1)"      "
```

72

```
6040 PRINTTAB(B)"    ":PRINTTAB(B-1)"      "
6050 PRINTTAB(B-2)"         "
6060 PRINTLEFT$(C$,K+4)
6070 PRINTTAB(B-2)"▓█ ▜▄▟ █  ██o"
6075 POKE54278,240
6080 POKEV1,15:POKEA1,9:FORT=1TO19:READS
     :READD:POKEW1,17:POKEH1,S:POKEH2,S
6090 FORTT=1TOD:NEXT:POKEW1,0:NEXT
6100 RESTORE
6110 CC=CC+1
6120 IFCC=10THENPRINT"▓▒▒YOU HAVE WON
     THE SHOW DOWN AGAINST 'VIC'":END
6125 IFYY=10THENPRINT"▓▒▒YOU HAVE LOST
     TO THE FASTEST GUN IN TOWN":END
6130 PRINT"◩":GOSUB10000
6140 GOTO400
9000 DATA200,360,220,360,200,240
9010 DATA180,120,150,360,150,240
9020 DATA100,120,150,240,160,120
9030 DATA180,720,200,360,130,360
9040 DATA200,360,195,360,200,240
9050 DATA210,120,205,240,200,120
9060 DATA190,480
9070 DATA-1
9100 REM****SPRITE DATA******
9110 DATA0,60,0,0,126,0,0,255,0,1,255,
     128,7,255,224,31,255,248,127,255,
     254
9120 DATA255,255,255,124,231,62,56,66,
     28,56,66,28,56,66,28,56,66,28
9130 DATA56,66,28,56,66,28,56,66,28,59,
     255,220,58,90,92,58,90,92
9140 DATA126,255,126,255,255,255
9150 DATA15,255,224,8,0,32,120,0,62,64,
     0,2,94,60,122,210,36,75,146,36,73
```

```
9160 DATA158,60,121,128,0,1,128,0,1,128
     ,0,1,131,231,193,130,36,65,130,36,65
9170 DATA131,231,193,128,0,1,128,0,1,159
     ,0,249,149,0,169,149,0,169,255,255,
     255
9180 DATA0,1,0,0,194,0,0,196,0,1,46,0,2,
     30,0,4,14,0,8,6,0,16,2,0,96,1,128
9190 DATA255,255,192,224,1,192,94,30,128
     ,82,18,128,82,210,128,82,210,128
9200 DATA82,210,128,94,222,128,224,1,192
     ,255,255,192,0,0,0,0,0,0
9210 DATA255,255,255,128,0,1,128,0,1,189
     ,231,189,165,36,165,165,36,165
9220 DATA189,231,189,128,0,1,128,0,1,128
     ,0,1,255,255,255,255,255,255,191,
     255,253
9230 DATA160,0,5,161,255,5,161,17,5,161,
     17,5,161,57,5,225,17,7,255,255,255
9240 DATA255,255,255
9250 DATA0,0,0,0,0,0,0,0,0,0,255,0,0,129
     ,0,14,165,112,234,153,87,187,129,221
9260 DATA128,0,1,191,189,253,191,189,253
     ,128,0,1,255,255,255,255,255,255
9270 DATA255,255,255,191,255,253,159,255
     ,249,136,153,17,156,153,57,255,255,255
9280 DATA255,255,255
9290 DATA0,255,0,1,129,128,3,255,192,6,0
     ,96,15,255,240,24,0,24,63,255,252
9300 DATA127,255,254,192,0,3,255,255,255
     ,129,1,1,157,1,121,149,1,73,149,1,
     73,149
9310 DATA239,73,149,41,73,149,239,73,149
     ,41,73,157,239,121,193,1,3,255,255,
     255
```

```
10000 Z=Z+1:IFZ=1THENPRINT"███████
      ██████████←██ ████
         ██████████ ████ ████████ "
10020 IFZ=2THENFORI=1044TO2023STEP40:
      POKEI,102:POKEI+54272,5:NEXT
10030 IFZ=3THENFORR=1TO20:ZZ=1024+INT
      (RND(1)*1000):POKEZZ,102:POKEZZ
      +54272,2:NEXT
10040 IFZ=4THENZ=0
10100 RETURN
```

READY.

```
0 REM**BULLET HEADS**   KEYBOARD VERSION
1 V1=54296:W1=54276:A1=54277:Q1=54278:
  H1=54273:H2=54272
2 POKEV1,15
3 FORA=1TO39:READS:NEXT
5 POKE2045,197:POKE650,128:DIMS(20),
  W(20)
6 POKE2040,192:POKE2041,193:POKE2042,
  194:POKE2043,195:POKE2044,196
7 FORH=192TO197
8 FORY=0TO62:READA:POKEH*64+Y,A:NEXTY,H
9 V=53248:POKEV+23,63:POKEV+29,63
10 POKEV+21,63:POKEV+39,15:POKEV+40,1:
   POKEV+41,1:POKEV+42,15:POKEV+43,15:
   POKEV+44,1
11 POKEV,70:POKEV+1,60:POKEV+4,36:POKE
   V+5,62:POKEV+2,120:POKEV+3,60
12 POKEV+8,200:POKEV+9,60:POKEV+6,250:
   POKEV+7,60
```

```
13 POKEV+16,32:POKEV+10,40:POKEV+11,60
18 PRINT"◻":X=30:L=7:SC=1024:CL=55296:
   K=13:B=3
19 RESTORE:GOSUB10000
20 A$="▓◻◻◻◻◻◻◻◻◻◻◻◻◻◻◻"
30 C$="▓◻◻◻◻◻◻◻◻◻◻◻◻◻◻◻"
400 PRINT"▓◻◻◻                            "
401 PRINT"▓◻◻◻OUTLAW VIC"YY:PRINT"▓"SPC
    (27)"◻SHERIFF"CC
402 IFOO=1THENPRINT"▓◻◻"SPC(24)"SHERIFF
    LOADING"
403 IFFF=1THENPRINT"▓◻◻OUTLAW VIC
    LOADING"
409 PRINTLEFT$(A$,L)
410 PRINTTAB(X)"     "
500 PRINTTAB(X)" ∩ ":PRINTTAB(X-3)" ∪ "
510 PRINTTAB(X-2)"  ◼◼, ◼, ":PRINTTAB
    (X-1)"  ◼◼ ◼ "
512 PRINTTAB(X)" ◼◼ ◼ ":PRINTTAB(X-1)"
    ◼◼◼ ◥"
519 PRINTTAB(X-2)"          "
520 GETB$:IFB$="I"THENL=L-1
530 IFB$="M"THENL=L+1
540 IFB$=" "ANDOO=0THEN999
550 IFL<7THENL=7
560 IFL>14THENL=14
570 IFOO=1THENJ=J+1:IFJ=5THENPP=0:OO=0
    :J=0
580 IFFF=1THENG=G+1:IFG=5THENDD=0:FF=0
    :G=0
600 PRINTLEFT$(A$,K)
610 PRINTTAB(B)"     "
620 PRINTTAB(B)" ∩ ":PRINTTAB(B-3)" ∪ "
630 PRINTTAB(B-2)"  ◼◼, ◼, ":PRINTTAB
    (B-1)"  ◼◼ ◼ "
640 PRINTTAB(B)" ◼◼ ◼ ":PRINTTAB(B-1)"
```

```
      ▄▀▀▄ ▚"
650 PRINTTAB(B-2)"          "
660 IFRND(1)>.65THENK=K+(K>L)-(K<L)
670 IFRND(1)>.6ANDFF=0THEN1999
680 IFK<7THENK=7
690 IFK>14THENK=14
700 GOTO400
999 PRINTLEFT$(A$,L)
1000 PP=PP+1:IFPP=6THENOO=1
1009 PRINTTAB(X)" ∩ "
1010 PRINTTAB(X)" ∪ "
1020 PRINTTAB(X-2)"▟▖▆  ▟▌ ▆ "
1030 PRINTTAB(X-1)"▛▙▟▖ ▆ "
1040 PRINTTAB(X+1)"▟▌  "
1050 PRINTTAB(X)"▆▄▟ ▆ "
1060 PRINTTAB(X-1)"▛▛▆ ▟▌▆▖▄"
1061 POKEW1,129:POKEA1,9:POKEQ1,240:POKE
     H1,40:POKEH2,200:FORYG=15TO0STEP-1
1062 POKEV1,YG:FORGY=1TO10:NEXTGY,YG:
     POKEQ1,0:POKEW1,0
1070 FORR=X-4TO0STEP-1:P=PEEK(SC+R+40*
     (L+2))
1071 IFP=102THENPOKESC+R+40*(L+2),32:
     POKESC+(R+1)+40*(L+2),32:GOTO400
1072 IFP<>32ANDP<>102THEN6000
1080 POKESC+R+40*(L+2),46:POKECL+R+40*
     (L+2),0:POKESC+(R+1)+40*(L+2),32
1090 NEXT:POKESC+(R+1)+40*(L+2),32:
     GOTO400
1999 PRINTLEFT$(C$,K)
2000 DD=DD+1:IFDD=6THENFF=1
2009 PRINTTAB(B)" ∩ "
2010 PRINTTAB(B)" ∪ "
2020 PRINTTAB(B)"▟▌ ▆  ▟▖▖"
2030 PRINTTAB(B)"▟▌ ▆▖▄▖▟▖▄"
```

```
2040 PRINTTAB(B)"▨█ █  "
2050 PRINTTAB(B)"██ ▟█▙  "
2060 PRINTTAB(B-1)"█▙▟ ▞█ ▟▜█  "
2065 PRINTTAB(B-1)"        "
2066 POKEW1,129:POKEA1,9:POKEQ1,240:POKE
2067 POKEV1,YG:FORGY=1TO10:NEXTGY,YG:
     POKEQ1,0:POKEW1,0
2070 FORR=B+5TO35:D=PEEK(SC+R+40*(K+2))
2071 IFD=102THENPOKESC+R+40*(K+2),32:
     POKESC+(R-1)+40*(K+2),32:GOTO400
2072 IFD<>32ANDD<>102THEN5000
2080 POKESC+R+40*(K+2),46:POKECL+R+40*
     (K+2),0:POKESC+(R-1)+40*(K+2),32
2090 NEXT:POKESC+(R-1)+40*(K+2),32:
     GOTO400
5000 PRINTLEFT$(A$,L)
5010 PRINTTAB(X)"    "
5020 PRINTTAB(X)"   ":PRINTTAB(X-3)"    "
5030 PRINTTAB(X-2)"      ":PRINTTAB(X-1)
     "     "
5040 PRINTTAB(X)"    ":PRINTTAB(X-1)"  "
5050 PRINTTAB(X-2)"     "
5060 PRINTLEFT$(C$,K+4)
5070 PRINTTAB(X-3)"O▨█ █ █▄▟"
5075 POKE54278,180
5080 POKEV1,15:POKEA1,9:FORT=1TO19:READS
     :READD:POKEW1,17:POKEH1,S:POKEH2,S
5090 FORTT=1TOD:NEXT:POKEW1,0:NEXT
5095 RESTORE
5100 YY=YY+1:GOTO6120
6000 PRINTLEFT$(A$,K)
6010 PRINTTAB(B)"    "
6020 PRINTTAB(B)"   ":PRINTTAB(B-3)"   "
6030 PRINTTAB(B-2)"      ":PRINTTAB
     (B-1)"     "
```

```
6040 PRINTTAB(B)"    ":PRINTTAB(B-1)"  "
6050 PRINTTAB(B-2)"      "
6060 PRINTLEFT$(C$,K+4)
6070 PRINTTAB(B-2)"▩▩ ▆▅▩ █  ██0"
6075 POKE54278,240
6080 POKEV1,15:POKEA1,9:FORT=1TO19:READS
     :READD:POKEW1,17:POKEH1,S:POKEH2,S
6090 FORTT=1TOD:NEXT:POKEW1,0:NEXT
6100 RESTORE
6110 CC=CC+1
6120 IFCC=10THENPRINT"▩▩▩YOU HAVE WON
     THE SHOW DOWN AGAINST 'VIC'":END
6125 IFYY=10THENPRINT"▩▩▩YOU HAVE LOST
     TO THE FASTEST GUN IN TOWN":END
6130 PRINT"▨":GOSUB10000
6140 GOTO400
9000 DATA200,360,200,360,200,240
9010 DATA180,120,150,360,150,240
9020 DATA100,120,150,240,160,120
9030 DATA180,720,200,360,190,360
9040 DATA200,360,195,360,200,240
9050 DATA210,120,205,240,200,120
9060 DATA190,480
9070 DATA-1
9100 REM****SPRITE DATA******
9110 DATA0,60,0,0,126,0,0,255,0,1,255,
     128,7,255,224,31,255,248,127,255,254
9120 DATA255,255,255,124,231,62,56,66,
     28,56,66,28,56,66,28,56,66,28
9130 DATA56,66,28,56,66,28,56,66,28,59,
     255,220,58,90,92,58,90,92
9140 DATA126,255,126,255,255,255
9150 DATA15,255,224,8,0,32,120,0,62,64,
     0,2,94,60,122,210,36,75,146,36,73
9160 DATA158,60,121,128,0,1,128,0,1,128
```

79

```
       ,0,1,131,231,193,130,36,65,130,36,65
9170 DATA131,231,193,128,0,1,128,0,1,
       159,0,249,149,0,169,149,0,169,255,
       255,255
9180 DATA0,1,0,0,194,0,0,196,0,1,46,0,2
       ,30,0,4,14,0,8,6,0,16,2,0,96,1,128
9190 DATA255,255,192,224,1,192,94,30,128
       ,82,18,128,82,210,128,82,210,128
9200 DATA82,210,128,94,222,128,224,1,
       192,255,255,192,0,0,0,0,0,0
9210 DATA255,255,255,128,0,1,128,0,1,
       189,231,189,165,36,165,165,36,165
9220 DATA189,231,189,128,0,1,128,0,1,
       128,0,1,255,255,255,255,255,255,191
       ,255,253
9230 DATA160,0,5,161,255,5,161,17,5,161,
       17,5,161,57,5,225,17,7,255,255,255
9240 DATA255,255,255
9250 DATA0,0,0,0,0,0,0,0,0,0,255,0,0,129
       ,0,14,165,112,234,153,87,187,129,221
9260 DATA128,0,1,191,189,253,191,189,
       253,128,0,1,255,255,255,255,255,255
9270 DATA255,255,255,191,255,253,159,
       255,249,136,153,17,156,153,57,255,
       255,255
9280 DATA255,255,255
9290 DATA0,255,0,1,129,128,3,255,192,6,
       0,96,15,255,240,24,0,24,63,255,252
9300 DATA127,255,254,192,0,3,255,255,
       255,129,1,1,157,1,121,149,1,73,149
       ,1,73,149
9310 DATA239,73,149,41,73,149,239,73,
       149,41,73,157,239,121,193,1,3,255,
       255,255
```

```
10000  Z=Z+1:IFZ=1THENPRINT"
       ███████████████████████████
       ███████████████████████████ "
10020  IFZ=2THENFORI=1044TO2023STEP40:
       POKEI,102:POKEI+54272,5:NEXT
10030  IFZ=3THENFORR=1TO20:ZZ=1024+INT
       (RND(1)*1000):POKEZZ,102:POKEZZ
       +54272,2:NEXT
10040  IFZ=4THENZ=0
10100  RETURN

READY.
```

YACKMAN

You appear at the top of a maze filled with dots.
You must move your Yackman around the maze,
eating dots to gain points.

But beware...hungry monsters lurk in the darkness,
waiting to gobble you up.

If you eat one of the red apples, then you'll be able
to eat the monsters, but only for a certain period of
time. Once this time is up, they'll go after you again.
Note that you can eat the monsters only when they
are purple.

Use the following controls in the keyboard version:
"W" to move up
"X" to move down
"A" to move left
"D" to move right

```
0  REM**YACKMAN**         JOYSTICK VERSION
1  U=5
2  V1=54296:W1=54276:A1=54277:H1=54273:
   H2=54272
3  POKE53281,0
5  POKE650,255
10 PRINT"◌":POKEV1,15:FORA=1TOU:C(A)=46:
   NEXT
50 PRINT"█▓▓▓▓▓▓▓▓▓▓▓▓▓▓▓▓▓▓▓▓▓▓▓▓▓":PRINT"
   ▓█.....................██"
60 PRINT"▓█●▓▓█. ▓▓█. ▓▓█. ▓▓█.
   ▓▓▓█●▓▓"
```

```
70 PRINT"█▓.▓█▓......▓█▓.▓█▓.▓█▓.....▓█▓
   .▓█"
75 PRINT"█▓.▓█▓.▓█████▓.▓█▓:▓█▓.▓█▓.▓████
   .▓█▓.▓█"
80 PRINT"█▓....................▓█"
85 PRINT"█▓.▓█▓.▓████▓.▓█▓....▓█▓.▓████▓.
   ▓█▓.▓█"
90 PRINT"█▓.▓█▓.....▓█▓.▓█▓.▓█▓.....▓█▓.
   ▓█"
95 PRINT"█▓.▓████▓.▓████▓....▓████▓.▓████▓.
   ▓█"
100 PRINT"█▓...................▓█"
105 PRINT"████▓...▓█▓..▓█▓..▓█▓..▓█▓...
    ▓████"
110 PRINT"█▓...▓█▓.▓█▓.▓███▓..▓███▓.▓█▓.
    ▓█▓...▓█"
115 PRINT"█▓.▓█▓...▓█▓.......▓██▓...▓█▓.
    ▓█"
120 PRINT"█...▓█▓...▓███▓..▓████▓...▓█▓...
    ▓█"
125 PRINT"████▓...▓█▓..▓█▓..▓█▓..▓█▓...
    ▓████"
130 PRINT"█▓...▓█▓.▓█▓.......▓█▓.▓█▓...
    ▓█"
135 PRINT"█▓.▓█▓.......▓████▓.......▓█▓.▓█"
140 PRINT"█▓...▓████▓.▓█▓.▓███▓.▓█▓.▓████
    ...▓█"
145 PRINT"████▓.▓█▓...........▓█▓.▓████"
150 PRINT"█▓...▓█▓.▓████▓..▓████▓.▓█▓...
    ▓█"
151 PRINT"██●▓█▓.▓█▓.▓█▓..▓█▓..▓█▓..▓█▓.
    ▓█▓.▓█●▓█"
155 PRINT"█▓....................▓█
    ":PRINT"████████████████████████████████"
```

84

```
160 SC=1024:CL=54272:X=1072:B=1:V=1
161 FORTR=1TO5:L(TR)=1:NEXT
170 DIMQ(5),W(5)
175 Q(3)=18:W(3)=1:Q(4)=11:W(4)=19:Q(5)=8
    :W(5)=16
180 Q(1)=11:W(1)=12:E=1:R=-1:Q(2)=2:W(2)
    =1
190 X=X-1:IFPEEK(X)=102THENX=X+1
195 GOSUB9000
200 P=PEEK(X):IFP=46THENGOSUB3000:S=S+1:
    IFS=279THEN2000
212 IFP=81THENGOSUB5000:B=0:V=5:TI$=
    "000000"
220 POKEX,41:POKECL+X,15
221 GOSUB610
225 POKEX,32
230 JV=PEEK(56320):JV=15-(JVAND15):
    IFJV=0THEN290
240 IFJV=4THEN190
250 IFJV=8THEN300
260 IFJV=1THEN410
270 IFJV=2THEN510
290 GOTO200
300 X=X+1:IFPEEK(X)=102THENX=X-1
305 GOSUB9000
310 P=PEEK(X):IFP=46THENGOSUB3000:S=S+1:
    IFS=279THEN2000
322 IFP=81THENGOSUB5000:B=0:V=5:
    TI$="000000"
330 POKEX,41:POKECL+X,15
334 GOSUB610
335 POKEX,32
340 JV=PEEK(56320):JV=15-(JVAND15):
    IFJV=0THEN400
350 IFJV=4THEN190
```

```
360  IFJV=8THEN300
370  IFJV=1THEN410
380  IFJV=2THEN510
400  GOTO310
410  X=X-40:IFPEEK(X)=102THENX=X+40
415  GOSUB9000
420  P=PEEK(X):IFP=46THENGOSUB3000:S=S+1:
     IFS=279THEN2000
432  IFP=81THENGOSUB5000:B=0:V=5:
     TI$="000000"
440  POKEX,41:POKECL+X,15
444  GOSUB610
445  POKEX,32
450  JV=PEEK(56320):JV=15-(JVAND15):
     IFJV=0THEN500
460  IFJV=4THEN190
470  IFJV=8THEN300
480  IFJV=1THEN410
490  'FJV=2THEN510
500  GOTO420
510  X=X+40:IFPEEK(X)=102THENX=X-40
515  GOSUB9000
520  P=PEEK(X):IFP=46THENGOSUB3000:S=S+1:
     IFS=279THEN2000
532  IFP=81THENGOSUB5000:B=0:V=5:
     TI$="000000"
540  POKEX,41:POKECL+X,15
544  GOSUB610
545  POKEX,32
550  JV=PEEK(56320):JV=15-(JVAND15):
     IFJV=0THEN600
560  IFJV=4THEN190
570  IFJV=8THEN300
580  IFJV=1THEN410
590  IFJV=2THEN510
```

```
600 GOTO510
610 FORA=1TOU:IFL(A)=0THEN675
611 L=INT(RND(1)*2)+1
612 POKESC+Q(A)+40*W(A),C(A)
613 IFB=0ANDTI$>"000013"THENPRINT
    "▓▓▓▓▓▓▓▓▓▓"SPC(24)
    "◼GHOSTS CHANGING"
620 IFL=1THENR=-R
628 IFL=2THENE=-E:GOTO650
629 POKEX,32
630 JV=PEEK(56320):JV=15-(JVAND15):
    IFJV=0THEN639
631 IFJV=4THENX=X-1:IFPEEK(X)=102
    THENX=X+1
632 IFJV=8THENX=X+1:IFPEEK(X)=102
    THENX=X-1
633 IFJV=1THENX=X-40:IFPEEK(X)=102
    THENX=X+40
634 IFJV=2THENX=X+40:IFPEEK(X)=102
    THENX=X-40
635 GOSUB9000
636 P=PEEK(X):IFP=46THENGOSUB3000:S=S+1:
    IFS=279THEN2000
637 IFP=81THENGOSUB5000:B=0:V=5:
    TI$="000000"
639 POKEX,41:POKEX+CL,15
640 Q(A)=Q(A)+R:IFPEEK(SC+Q(A)+40*W
    (A))=102THENQ(A)=Q(A)-R
650 W(A)=W(A)+E:IFPEEK(SC+Q(A)+40*W
    (A))=102THENW(A)=W(A)-E
655 IFPEEK(SC+Q(A)+40*W(A))=46THENC(A)=46
656 IFPEEK(SC+Q(A)+40*W(A))=32THENC(A)=32
657 IFPEEK(SC+Q(A)+40*W(A))=81THENC(A)=81
659 POKESC+Q(A)+40*W(A),65:POKE55296+Q
```

```
         ( A )+40*W( A ),V
 660  JV=PEEK(56320):JV=15-(JVAND15):
      IFJV=0THEN669
 661  POKEX,32
 662  IFJV=4THENX=X-1:IFPEEK(X)=102
      THENX=X+1
 663  IFJV=8THENX=X+1:IFPEEK(X)=102
      THENX=X-1
 664  IFJV=1THENX=X-40:IFPEEK(X)=102
      THENX=X+40
 665  IFJV=2THENX=X+40:IFPEEK(X)=102
      THENX=X-40
 666  GOSUB9000
 667  P=PEEK(X):IFP=46THENGOSUB3000:S=S+1:
      IFS=279THEN2000
 668  IFP=81THENGOSUB5000:B=0:V=5:
      TI$="000000"
 669  POKEX,41:POKEX+CL,15
 670  IFSC+Q( A )+40*W( A )=XANDB=1THEN2000
 671  IFSC+Q( A )+40*W( A )=XANDB=0THENH=H+100
 672  IFV=5ANDTI$>"000015"THENGOSUB6000:
      B=1:V=1:FORTR=1TO5:L( TR )=1:NEXT
 673  IFB=0ANDTI$>"000013"THENPRINT
      "██████████████"SPC( 24 )"GHOSTS  CHANGING"
 675  NEXT
 680  RETURN
2000  POKEX,32:POKE650,0:PRINT"███████████
      ████████████████████████████████
      GAME OVER!! "
2005  FORA=1TO5:POKE53281,10:FORB=1TO500:
      NEXT:POKE53281,0:FORB=1TO500:NEXTB,A
2010  PRINT"███████████████████████████████
      SCORE"S*U+H
2020  END
3000  POKEV1,15:POKEW1,17:POKEA1,9
```

88

```
3010 POKEH1,17:POKEH2,37:FORYT=1TO10:
     NEXT:POKEW1,0:RETURN
5000 POKEV1,15:POKEW1,17:POKEA1,9
5010 FORTG=200TO255:POKEW1,17:POKEH1,TG:
     POKEH2,TG:POKEW1,0:NEXT
5020 FORTG=255TO200STEP-1:POKEW1,17:
     POKEH1,TG:POKEH2,TG:POKEW1,0:NEXT
5030 RETURN
6000 FORTY=1TO5:IFL(TY)=1THEN6040
6020 Q(TY)=P(TY):W(TY)=PP(TY)
6040 NEXT
6050 PRINT"◼◼◼◼◼◼◼◼◼◼◼◼◼"SPC(24)" ":RETURN
9000 IFB=0THEN9030
9010 FORTR=1TO5:IFX=SC+Q(TR)+40*W(TR)
     THEN2000
9020 NEXT:RETURN
9030 FORTR=1TO5:IFX=SC+Q(TR)+40*W(TR)
     THENH=H+100:L(TR)=0:GOSUB9050
9040 NEXT:RETURN
9050 POKEV1,15:POKEW1,17:POKEA1,9:
     POKESC+Q(TR)+40*W(TR),C(TY):P(TR)=Q
     (TR)
9055 PP(TR)=W(TR):Q(TR)=0:W(TR)=0
9060 FORTG=100TO150:POKEW1,17:POKEH1,TG:
     POKEH2,TG:POKEW1,0:NEXT:RETURN

     READY.


_____


0 REM**YACKMAN**        KEYBOARD VERSION
1 U=5
2 V1=54296:W1=54276:A1=54277:H1=54273:
  H2=54272
```

```
3 POKE53281,0
5 POKE650,255
10 PRINT"◻":POKEV1,15:FORA=1TOU:C(A)=46:
   NEXT
50 PRINT"▨▪■████████████████████████████":
   PRINT"▨◰............................◰▨"
60 PRINT"▨◰●▨████◰.◰███◰.◰███◰.◰█████◰.◰█████
   ●◰▨"
70 PRINT"▨◰.◰█◰.....◰██◰.◰██◰.◰██◰.....
   ◰██◰.◰▨"
75 PRINT"▨◰.◰█◰.◰█████◰.◰█◰.◰███◰.◰██◰.
   ◰█████◰.◰█◰.◰▨"
80 PRINT"▨◰.....................◰▨"
85 PRINT"▨◰.◰██◰.◰█████◰.◰██◰....◰██◰.◰█████◰.
   ◰██◰.◰▨"
90 PRINT"▨◰.◰██◰.....◰██◰.◰███◰.◰██◰.....
   ◰██◰.◰▨"
95 PRINT"▨◰.◰█████◰.◰██◰....◰█████◰.◰█████◰.
   ◰▨"
100 PRINT"▨◰.....................◰▨"
105 PRINT"▨████◰...◰██◰..◰██◰..◰██◰..◰██◰...
   ◰█████"
110 PRINT"▨◰...◰██◰.◰██◰.◰███◰..◰███◰.◰██◰.
   ◰██◰...◰▨"
115 PRINT"▨◰.◰██◰...◰██◰.......◰██◰...◰██◰.
   ◰▨"
120 PRINT"▨...◰██◰...◰███◰..◰███◰...◰██◰...
   ◰▨"
125 PRINT"▨████◰...◰██◰..◰██◰..◰██◰..◰██◰...
   ◰█████"
130 PRINT"▨◰...◰██◰.◰██◰.......◰██◰.◰██◰...
   ◰▨"
135 PRINT"▨◰.◰██◰.......◰████◰.......◰██◰.◰▨"
```

90

```
140 PRINT"██....██████.██.████.██.
    ██████...██"
145 PRINT"██████.████............███.██████"
150 PRINT"██...██. ██████...██████.██...
    ██"
151 PRINT"██●██. ██. ████...██...██...██.
    ██. ██●██"
155 PRINT"██....................██
    ":PRINT"████████████████████████████████"
160 SC=1024:CL=54272:X=1072:B=1:V=1
161 FORTR=1TO5:L(TR)=1:NEXT
170 DIMQ(5),W(5)
175 Q(3)=18:W(3)=1:Q(4)=11:W(4)=19:Q(5)=8
    :W(5)=16
180 Q(1)=11:W(1)=12:E=1:R=-1:Q(2)=2:W
    (2)=1
190 X=X-1:IFPEEK(X)=102THENX=X+1
195 GOSUB9000
200 P=PEEK(X):IFP=46THENGOSUB3000:S=S+1:
    IFS=279THEN2000
212 IFP=81THENGOSUB5000:B=0:V=5:
    TI$="000000"
220 POKEX,41:POKECL+X,15
221 GOSUB610
225 POKEX,32
230 GETA$:IFA$=""THEN290
240 IFA$="A"THEN190
250 IFA$="D"THEN300
260 IFA$="W"THEN410
270 IFA$="X"THEN510
290 GOTO200
300 X=X+1:IFPEEK(X)=102THENX=X-1
305 GOSUB9000
310 P=PEEK(X):IFP=46THENGOSUB3000:S=S+1:
    IFS=279THEN2000
```

91

```
322  IFP=81THENGOSUB5000:B=0:V=5:
     TI$="000000"
330  POKEX,41:POKECL+X,15
334  GOSUB610
335  POKEX,32
340  GETA$:IFA$=""THEN400
350  IFA$="A"THEN190
360  IFA$="D"THEN300
370  IFA$="W"THEN410
380  IFA$="X"THEN510
400  GOTO310
410  X=X-40:IFPEEK(X)=102THENX=X+40
415  GOSUB9000
420  P=PEEK(X):IFP=46THENGOSUB3000:S=S+1:
     IFS=279THEN2000
432  IFP=81THENGOSUB5000:B=0:V=5:
     TI$="000000"
440  POKEX,41:POKECL+X,15
444  GOSUB610
445  POKEX,32
450  GETA$:IFA$=""THEN500
460  IFA$="A"THEN190
470  IFA$="D"THEN300
480  IFA$="W"THEN410
490  IFA$="X"THEN510
500  GOTO420
510  X=X+40:IFPEEK(X)=102THENX=X-40
515  GOSUB9000
520  P=PEEK(X):IFP=46THENGOSUB3000:S=S+1:
     IFS=279THEN2000
532  IFP=81THENGOSUB5000:B=0:V=5:
     TI$="000000"
540  POKEX,41:POKECL+X,15
544  GOSUB610
545  POKEX,32
550  GETA$:IFA$=""THEN600
```

```
560 IFA$="A"THEN190
570 IFA$="D"THEN300
580 IFA$="W"THEN410
590 IFA$="X"THEN510
600 GOTO510
610 FORA=1TOU:IFL(A)=0THEN675
611 L=INT(RND(1)*2)+1
612 POKESC+Q(A)+40*W(A),C(A)
613 IFB=0ANDTI$>"000013"THENPRINT"
    ░░░░░░░░░░░"SPC(24)"░GHOSTS CHANGING"
620 IFL=1THENR=-R
628 IFL :2THENE=-E:GOTO650
629 POKEX,32
630 GETA$:IFA$=""THEN639
631 IFA$="A"THENX=X-1:IFPEEK(X)=102
    THENX=X+1
632 IFA$="D"THENX=X+1:IFPEEK(X)=102
    THENX=X-1
633 IFA$="W"THENX=X-40:IFPEEK(X)=102
    THENX=X+40
634 IFA$="X"THENX=X+40:IFPEEK(X)=102
    THENX=X-40
635 GOSUB9000
636 P=PEEK(X):IFP=46THENGOSUB3000:S=S+1:
    IFS=279THEN2000
637 IFP=81THENGOSUB5000:B=0:V=5:
    TI$="000000"
639 POKEX,41:POKEX+CL,15
640 Q(A)=Q(A)+R:IFPEEK(SC+Q(A)+40*W
    (A))=102THENQ(A)=Q(A)-R
650 W(A)=W(A)+E:IFPEEK(SC+Q(A)+40*W
    (A))=102THENW(A)=W(A)-E
655 IFPEEK(SC+Q(A)+40*W(A))=46THENC(A)=46
656 IFPEEK(SC+Q(A)+40*W(A))=32THENC(A)=32
657 IFPEEK(SC+Q(A)+40*W(A))=81THENC(A)=81
```

93

```
659 POKESC+Q(A)+40*W(A),65:POKE55296+Q
    (A)+40*W(A),.
660 GETA$:IFA$=""THEN669
661 POKEX,32
662 IFA$="A"THENX=X-1:IFPEEK(X)=102
    THENX=X+1
663 IFA$="D"THENX=X+1:IFPEEK(X)=102
    THENX=X-1
664 IFA$="W"THENX=X-40:IFPEEK(X)=102
    THENX=X+40
665 IFA$="X"THENX=X+40:IFPEEK(X)=102
    THENX=X-40
666 GOSUB9000
667 P=PEEK(X):IFP=46THENGOSUB3000:S=S+1:
    IFS=279THEN2000
668 IFP=81THENGOSUB5000:B=0:V=5:
    TI$="000000"
669 POKEX,41:POKEX+CL,15
670 IFSC+Q(A)+40*W(A)=XANDB=1THEN2000
671 IFSC+Q(A)+40*W(A)=XANDB=0THENH=H+100
672 IFV=5ANDTI$>"000015"THENGOSUB6000:
    B=1:V=1:FORTR=1TO5:L(TR)=1:NEXT
673 IFB=0ANDTI$>"000013"THENPRINT
    "█████████████"SPC(24)"GHOSTS CHANGING"
675 NEXT
680 RETURN
2000 POKEX,32:POKE650,0:PRINT
"████████████████████████████████████████████
    GAME OVER!! "
2005 FORA=1TO5:POKE53281,10:FORB=1TO500:
    NEXT:POKE53281,0:FORB=1TO500:NEXTB,A
2010 PRINT"████████████████████████████████
    SCORE"S*U+H
2020 END
3000 POKEV1,15:POKEW1,17:POKEA1,9
```

94

```
3010 POKEH1,17:POKEH2,37:FORYT=1TO10:
     NEXT:POKEW1,0:RETURN
5000 POKEV1,15:POKEW1,17:POKEA1,9
5010 FORTG=200TO255:POKEW1,17:POKEH1,TG:
     POKEH2,TG:POKEW1,0:NEXT
5020 FORTG=255TO200STEP-1:POKEW1,17:
     POKEH1,TG:POKEH2,TG:POKEW1,0:NEXT
5030 RETURN
6000 FORTY=1TO5:IFL(TY)=1THEN6040
6020 Q(TY)=P(TY):W(TY)=PP(TY)
6040 NEXT
6050 PRINT"█████████████"SPC(24)" ":RETURN
9000 IFB=0THEN9030
9010 FORTR=1TO5:IFX=SC+Q(TR)+40*W(TR)
     THEN2000
9020 NEXT:RETURN
9030 FORTR=1TO5:IFX=SC+Q(TR)+40*W(TR)
     THENH=H+100:L(TR)=0:GOSUB9050
9040 NEXT:RETURN
9050 POKEV1,15:POKEW1,17:POKEA1,9:
     POKESC+Q(TR)+40*W(TR),C(TY):P(TR)=Q
     (TR)
9055 PP(TR)=W(TR):Q(TR)=0:W(TR)=0
9060 FORTG=100TO150:POKEW1,17:POKEH1,TG:
     POKEH2,TG:POKEW1,0:NEXT:RETURN


     READY.
```

GALAXY ROBBERS

In this game, you have to try and rid the galaxy of the Star Fighters. As they come into sight, your on-board computer will tell you to fire.

Your computer also gives you fuel readings, damage reports, a power reading, and tells you how many fighters you have hit.

The game ends when your fuel reaches 3000, or if you sustain 100% damage to your ship, or if you manage to rid the galaxy of 15 Star Fighters. In the keyboard version, the space bar fires your laser cannon, while you use the fire button to do this in the joystick version.

```
0  REM**GALAXY ROBBERS** JOYSTICK VERSION
1  V1=54296:W1=54276:A1=54272:H1=54273:
   H2=54272
5  Q(1)=1064:Q(2)=1072:Q(3)=1082
6  T$="
   ▓▧\▧\▧\▧\▧\▧\▧\▧\_____/▢/▢/▢/▢/▢/▢/▢/
7  TT$="▓▓▓▓▓▓▓▓▓▓▓▓ ▐▐▐▐▐▐▐    ▎▓▓▓▓▓▓▓
   ▐▐▐▐▐/▓▓▓/▐▐▐/▓▓▓/▐▐▐/▐▐▐/▓▓▓▓▓▓▐▐▐▐▐\▧\▧
   \▧\▧\"
100 POKEV1,15
110 SC=1024:CO=54272
120 S$="▓▓\▧\▧\▧\▧\▧\▧\▧\▧\▧\▧\/▢/▢/▢/▢
    /▢/▢/▢/▢/▢/"
130 SS$="▓▓ ▧ ▧ ▧ ▧ ▧ ▧ ▧ ▧ ▧ ▧ ▢ ▢ ▢ ▢
    ▢ ▢ ▢ ▢ ▢ ▢ "
```

96

```basic
140 PRINT"◻":POKE53281,0
160 PRINT"▒▓▒**STARSHIP GALAXY II**"
185 PRINT"▨▨▨▨▨▨▨▨▨▨▨▨▨"
190 PRINT"▨▨▨▨▓——COMPUTER——STATUS——"
191 PRINT"▨ FUEL:                    "
192 PRINT"▨POWER %                  "
193 PRINT"▨DAMAGE %                  "
194 PRINT"▨FIGHTERS HIT              "
195 PRINT"▨CONDITION:▓GREEN▨         "
196 PRINT"▨                          "
210 PRINT
    "▨◻◻◻◻◻◻◻◻◻◻◻◻◻◻◻◻◻◻◻◻◻◻◻◻◻▮▮▮▮▮▮▮▮▮R▨
    ":F=F+INT(RND(1)*10)
211 IFF>3000THEN5050
212 PRINT"▨◻◻◻◻◻◻◻◻◻◻◻◻◻◻◻◻◻◻R FUEL:"F:
    PRINT"▨POWER %"P:PRINT"▨DAMAGE %"D
213 PRINT"▨FIGHTERS HIT '"FH"'"
215 PRINTT$:PRINTTT$
220 IFQ<=1THENPRINT"▨◻◻◻◻◻◻◻◻◻◻◻◻◻◻◻◻◻
    ◻◻▮▮▮▮▮▮▮▮R▮GREEN"
221 IFQ=3THENPRINT"▨◻◻◻◻◻◻◻◻◻◻◻◻◻◻◻◻◻◻◻
    ◻▮▮▮▮▮▮▮▮R▮RED▨   "
230 IFQ=2THENPRINT"▨◻◻◻◻◻◻◻◻◻◻◻◻◻◻◻◻◻◻◻
    ◻▮▮▮▮▮▮▮▮R▮AMBER"
235 FORR=1TOQ:IFQ(R)<1394ORQ(R)>1396
    THEN239
236 IFQ(R)>1393ANDQ(R)<1396THENPRINT"▨◻◻
    ◻◻◻◻◻◻◻◻◻◻▮▮▮▮▮▮▮A ▨▮FIRE▮| "
237 IFQ(R)>1393ANDQ(R)<1396THENPRINT
    "▨◻◻◻◻◻◻◻◻◻◻◻▮▮▮▮▮▮▮A ▨▮FIRE▮| "
238 FORI1=1TO100:NEXT
239 NEXT
240 JV=PEEK(56320):FR=JVAND16:JV=15-
    (JVAND15):IFJV=0ANDFR=16THEN270
```

98

```
250 IFFR=0THEN2800
260 GOTO210
270 IFRND(1)>.9THENQ=Q+1
275 IFQ>3THENQ=3
300 FORR=1TOQ:POKEQ(R),32:POKEQ(R)+1,32:
    POKEQ(R)+2,32
305 IFRND(1)>.95THENGOSUB5000
310 Q(R)=Q(R)+INT(RND(1)*3+39)
320 IFQ(R)>1624THENQ(R)=1064+INT(RND(1)*
    20)+1
330 POKEQ(R),225:POKEQ(R)+1,64:POKEQ
  (R)+2,97:POKEQ(R)+CO,1:POKEQ(R)+1+CO,1
340 POKEQ(R)+2+CO,1:NEXT
350 IFQ(R)=14340RQ(R)=14330RQ(R)=14320RQ
    (R)=1431THEN2000
360 GOTO210
2000 REM
2010 FORR=1TO3:POKEQ(R),32:POKEQ
    (R)+1,32:POKEQ(R)+2,32:NEXT
2020 Q=Q-1:GOTO210
2800 P=P+INT(RND(1)*10):IFP>=1000THE
    NP=1000:GOTO260
2900 PRINTS$:POKEA1,9:FORR=128TO255STE
    P7:POKEW1,17:POKEH1,R:POKEH2,R:
    POKEW1,0:NE XT
2910 FORR=1TOQ:IFQ(R)=14340RQ(R)=14330RQ
    (R)=14320RQ(R)=1431THEN3015
2920 NEXT
3000 PRINTSS$:GOTO260
3015 PRINTSS$:POKEV1,15
3020 POKEQ(R)+1,160:POKEQ(R)-40,127:POKE
    Q(R)-38,255:POKEQ(R)+40,255:POKEQ
    (R)+42,
127
3025 POKEQ(R),32:POKEQ(R)+2,32
3030 POKEQ(R)+1+CO,5:POKEQ(R)-40+CO,7:
```

```
         POKEQ(R)-38+CO,7:POKEQ(R)+40+CO,7:
         POKEQ(R)+42+CO,7
3031  POKE54278,240:POKEW1,129:POKEH1,40:
         POKEH2,200:FORYG=15TO0STEP-1:
         POKEV1,YG
3032  FORGY=1TO20:NEXTGY,YG
3033  POKE54278,0:POKEW1,0:POKEV1,15
3040  FH=FH+1:Q=Q-1
3050  S=S+1:IFS=15THENPRINT"▨◧◪YOU HAVE
         COMPLETED    YOUR MISSION":END
3060  Q(R)=1064+INT(RND(1)*20)+1:GOTO2000
5000  FORI=255TO128STEP-8:POKEW1,17:POKEH
         1,I:POKEH2,I:POKEW1,0:NEXT
5004  POKEQ(R),32:POKEQ(R)+1,32:POKEQ
         (R)+2,32
5005  POKEQ(R)+1,46:FORI1=1TO350:NEXT:
         POKEQ(R)+1,32:POKEQ(R)+2,123:FOR
         I1=1TO350:NEXT
5006  POKEQ(R)+2,32:POKEQ(R)+1,160:FOR
         I1=1TO350:NEXT:POKEQ(R)+1,32
5007  POKEQ(R)+2,32
5010  IFRND(1)<.7THENRETURN
5020  POKE53281,2:POKE53280,0
5021  POKE54278,240:POKEW1,129:POKEH1,40:
         POKEH2,200:FORYG=15TO0STEP-1:POKEV1
         ,YG
5022  FORGY=1TO20:NEXTGY,YG:POKEW1,0:
         POKE54278,0:POKEV1,15
5040  POKEV1,15:D=D+INT(RND(1)*10)+1
5050  IFD>=1000RF>3000THENPRINT"▨◧◪YOU
         FAILED":END
5060  POKE53281,0:POKE53280,14:RETURN

READY.
```

```
0 REM**GALAXY ROBBERS**.KEYBOARD VERSION
1 V1=54296:W1=54276:A1=54272:H1=54273:
  H2=54272
5 Q(1)=1064:Q(2)=1072:Q(3)=1082
6 T$="███\█\█\█\█\█\█\█\█\█\_____/�/system/system/system/system
  /system/system/system/
7 TT$="███████████████████████████
       | █████████   ██████/████/████/████/████/
       ████████████████\█\█\█\█\"
100 POKEV1,15
110 SC=1024:CO=54272
120 S$="███\ \█\█\█\█\█\█\█\█\█\█\█\/system/system/system/
       system/system/system/system/system/"
130 SS$="███ █ █ █ █ █ █ █ █ █ █
            □ □ □ □ □ □ □ □ □ □ □ "
140 PRINT"◻":POKE53281,0
160 PRINT"███**STARSHIP GALAXY II**"
185 PRINT"█████████████████"
190 PRINT"███████----COMPUTER----STATUS----"
191 PRINT"█▲FUEL:                      "
192 PRINT"█POWER %                  "
193 PRINT"█DAMAGE %                  "
194 PRINT"█FIGHTERS HIT              "
195 PRINT"█CONDITION:█GREEN▲         "
196 PRINT"█                         "
210 PRINT"█████████████████████████████████████████
       █████            ":F=F+INT(RND(1)*10)
211 IFF>3000THEN5050
212 PRINT"████████████████████████R FUEL:"F:
       PRINT"█POWER %"P:PRINT"█DAMAGE %"D
213 PRINT"█FIGHTERS HIT '"FH"'"
215 PRINTTT$:PRINTTT$
220 IFQ<=1THENPRINT"██████████████████████████████
```

101

```
                    ████████████████R↑GREEN"
221 IFQ=3THENPRINT"██████████████████████████
    ████████████R£RED█    "
230 IFQ=2THENPRINT"███████████████████████████
    ████████████R£AMBER"
235 FORR=1TOQ:IFQ(R)<1394ORQ(R)>1396
    THEN239
236 IFQ(R)>1393ANDQ(R)<1396THENPRINT"
    ███████████████████████ R£FIRE█| "
237 IFQ(R)>1393ANDQ(R)<1396THENPRINT"
    ███████████████████████ R£FIRE█| "
238 FORI1=1TO100:NEXT
239 NEXT
240 GETA$:IFA$=""THEN270
250 IFA$=" "THEN2800
260 GOTO210
270 IFRND(1)>.9THENQ=Q+1
275 IFQ>3THENQ=3
300 FORR=1TOQ:POKEQ(R),32:POKEQ(R)+1,32
    :POKEQ(R)+2,32
305 IFRND(1)>.95THENGOSUB5000
310 Q(R)=Q(R)+INT(RND(1)*3+39)
320 IFQ(R)>1624THENQ(R)=1064+INT(RND(1)
    *20)+1
330 POKEQ(R),225:POKEQ(R)+1,64:POKEQ(R)
    +2,97:POKEQ(R)+CO,1:POKEQ(R)+1+CO,1
340 POKEQ(R)+2+CO,1:NEXT
350 IFQ(R)=1434ORQ(R)=1433ORQ(R)=1432OR
    Q(R)=1431THEN2000
360 GOTO210
2000 REM
2010 FORR=1TO3:POKEQ(R),32:POKEQ(R)+1,
    32:POKEQ(R)+2,32:NEXT
2020 Q=Q-1:GOTO210
2800 P=P+INT(RND(1)*10):IFP>=1000THENP=
    1000:GOTO260
```

102

```
2900 PRINTS$:POKEA1,9:FORR=128TO255STEP7
     :POKEW1,17:POKEH1,R:POKEH2,R:POKEW1
     ,0:NEXT
2910 FORR=1TOQ:IFQ(R)=1434ORQ(R)=1433ORQ
     (R)=1432ORQ(R)=1431THEN3015
2920 NEXT
3000 PRINTSS$:GOTO260
3015 PRINTSS$:POKEV1,15
3020 POKEQ(R)+1,160:POKEQ(R)-40,127:POKE
     Q(R)-38,255:POKEQ(R)+40,255:POKEQ
     (R)+42,127
3025 POKEQ(R),32:POKEQ(R)+2,32
3030 POKEQ(R)+1+CO,5:POKEQ(R)-40+CO,7:
     POKEQ(R)-38+CO,7:POKEQ(R)+40+CO,7:
     POKEQ(R)+42+CO,7
3031 POKE54278,240:POKEW1,129:POKEH1,40
     :POKEH2,200:FORYG=15TO0STEP-1:POKE
     V1,YG
3032 FORGY=1TO20:NEXTGY,YG
3033 POKE54278,0:POKEW1,0:POKEV1,15
3040 FH=FH+1:Q=Q-1
3050 S=S+1:IFS=15THENPRINT"   YOU HAVE
     COMPLETED    YOUR MISSION":END
3060 Q(R)=1064+INT(RND(1)*20)+1:GOTO2000
5000 FORI=255TO128STEP-8:POKEW1,17:POKE
     H1,I:POKEH2,I:POKEW1,0:NEXT
5004 POKEQ(R),32:POKEQ(R)+1,32:POKEQ(R)
     +2,32
5005 POKEQ(R)+1,46:FORI1=1TO350:NEXT:
     POKEQ(R)+1,32:POKEQ(R)+2,123:FORI1
     =1TO350:NEXT
5006 POKEQ(R)+2,32:POKEQ(R)+1,160:FORI1
     =1TO350:NEXT:POKEQ(R)+1,32
5007 POKEQ(R)+2,32
5010 IFRND(1)<.7THENRETURN
5020 POKE53281,2:POKE53280,0
```

```
5021 POKE54278,240:POKEW1,129:POKEH1,40:
     POKEH2,200:FORYG=15TO0STEP-1:POKEV
     1,YG
5022 FORGY=1TO20:NEXTGY,YG:POKEW1,0:POKE
     54278,0:POKEV1,15
5040 POKEV1,15:D=D+INT(RND(1)*10)+1
5050 IFD>=1000RF>3000THENPRINT"█R YOU
     FAILED":END
5060 POKE53281,0:POKE53280,14:RETURN

READY.
```

SPRITE CREATION

This program is more of a very useful 'tool' than a game. It is invaluable for helping you defining sprite graphics. Here's the steps you follow:

1. You use the cursor keys to draw your sprite.
2. You use the function keys for sketching and rub-out.
3. After you've created your sprite, you'll be able to view it and have it enlarged.
4. Next you'll be given the DATA which you can either (a) copy down by hand, or (b) have the computer dump to the printer.

Note that you can use a joystick to define your sprites. In this case, you need to press the 'FIRE' button to sketch and rub-out. Full instructions are included in the program.

```
1 REM**SPRITE CREATION** JOYSTICK VERSION
5 DIMQ(22),W(22),E(22)
10 PRINT"◻":SC=1024:A=0:B=0:CL=55296
11 PRINT"▓▓▓▓▓▓▓▓▓▓▓▓▓▓▓▓▓▓▓▓▓▓▓▓▓──
   ──────────"
12 PRINT"▓▓▓▓▓▓▓▓▓▓▓▓▓▓▓▓▓▓▓▓▓▓▓▓
   —SPRITE CREATER—"
13 PRINT"▓▓▓▓▓▓▓▓▓▓▓▓▓▓▓▓▓▓▓▓▓▓▓▓▓──
   ──────────"
14 PRINT"▓▓▓▓▓▓▓▓▓▓▓▓▓▓▓▓▓▓▓▓▓▓▓▓▓'R'
   TO RE-RUN.."
15 PRINT"▓▓▓▓▓▓▓▓▓▓▓▓▓▓▓▓▓▓▓▓▓▓▓▓▓
   'FIRE BUTTON' TO"
```

```
16 PRINT"█████████████████████████████
   SKETCH & RUBOUT"
17 PRINT"██████████████████████████████
   'RETURN'  DATA.."
18 PRINT"██████████████████████████████
   'Q' TO QUITE"
20 JV=PEEK(56320):FR=JVAND16:
   JV=15-(JVAND15)
25 GETA$
30 IFA$="R"THENGOTO10
35 IFA$="Q"THEN2370
40 IFJV=1THENB=B-1
50 IFJV=2THENB=B+1
60 IFJV=4THENA=A-1
70 IFJV=8THENA=A+1
80 IFA$=CHR$(13)THENGOTO2000
81 IFZ=0ANDFR=0THENZ=1:GOTO90
82 IFZ=1ANDFR=0THENZ=0
90 IFB<0THENB=0
100 IFB>20THENB=20
110 IFA<0THENA=0
120 IFA>23THENA=23
130 IFZ=0THENPOKESC+A+40*B,32:FORT=1TO30:
    NEXT:POKESC+A+40*B,160:POKECL+A+40
    *B,1
131 IFZ=1THENPOKESC+A+40*B,160:POKECL+A+
    40*B,13:FORT=1TO30:NEXT:POKESC+A+40
    *B,32
140 GOTO20
2000 REM********
2010 REM*DECODE*
2020 REM********
2021 PRINT"████████████████████████████
     ████STAGE# 1"
2030 FORT=1TO21
```

107

```
2031 IFT=1THEN2090
2032 SC=SC+40
2090 FORR=0TO7
2100 IFPEEK(SC+R)=160THENGOSUB5000
2110 NEXT
2120 NEXT
2121 PRINT"███████████████████████████████
     ███STAGE#2"
2130 SC=1032'
2140 FORT=1TO21:IFT=1THEN2160
2150 SC=SC+40
2160 FORR=0TO7
2170 IFPEEK(SC+R)=160THENGOSUB6000
2180 NEXT
2190 NEXT
2191 PRINT"███████████████████████████████
     ███FINAL STAGE"
2200 SC=1040
2210 FORT=1TO21:IFT=1THEN2230
2220 SC=SC+40
2230 FORR=0TO7
2240 IFPEEK(SC+R)=160THENGOSUB7000
2250 NEXT
2260 NEXT
2265 GOTO2341
2270 PRINT"▨─────────────────────────────
     ─            DATA"
2280 PRINT"──────────────────────────────────────"
2290 PRINT"DO YOU WANT TO SEND THE DATA
     TO THE ▨P▉RINTER OR ▨W▉RITE IT DOWN"
2291 INPUTA$:IFA$="P"THENOPEN4,4:CMD4
2300 PRINT"▨":FORT=1TO21
2310 PRINT"DATA"Q(T)","W(T)","E(T)
2320 NEXT
```

108

```
2322 IFA$="P"THENPRINT#4:CLOSE4:PRINT"◨"
2330 PRINT"◙◲HIT 'RETURN' TO CONTINUE"
2339 GETA$:IFA$<>CHR$(13)THEN2339
2340 GOTO2350
2341 PRINT"◳WOULD YOU LIKE TO VIEW
     YOUR SPRITE"
2342 INPUTA$:IFA$="Y"THEN3000
2343 GOTO2270
2350 PRINT"◳WOULD YOU LIKE TO CREATE
     ANOTHER SPRITE"
2351 FORN=0TO62:POKE832+N,0:NEXT:N=0
2360 INPUTA$:IFA$="Y"THENRUN
2362 IFA$="N"THEN2370
2366 GOTO10
2370 PRINT"◳YOU HAVE BEEN USING THE
     'SPRITE CREATER'":END
3000 V=53248:POKEV+21,4:POKE2042,13
3002 D=832:POKEV+23,0:POKEV+29,0
3003 POKEV+4,200:POKEV+5,200
3010 FORTT=1TO21
3020 POKED,Q(TT):POKED+1,W(TT)
     :POKED+2,E(TT):D=D+3:NEXT
3050 PRINT"◳DO YOU WANT YOUR SPRITE
     ENLARGED"
3051 INPUTA$:IFA$="Y"THENPOKEV+23,4:
     POKEV+29,4
3055 PRINT"◨"
3059 FORX=0TO200:POKEV+4,X:POKEV+5,X
     :NEXT
3060 PRINT"◳HIT 'RETURN' TO CONTINUE"
3070 GETA$:IFA$<>CHR$(13)THEN3070
3080 GOTO2270
5000 IFR=0THENQ(T)=Q(T)+128
```

109

```
5010  IFR=1THENQ(T)=Q(T)+64
5020  IFR=2THENQ(T)=Q(T)+32
5030  IFR=3THENQ(T)=Q(T)+16
5040  IFR=4THENQ(T)=Q(T)+8
5050  IFR=5THENQ(T)=Q(T)+4
5060  IFR=6THENQ(T)=Q(T)+2
5070  IFR=7THENQ(T)=Q(T)+1
5080  RETURN
6000  IFR=0THENW(T)=W(T)+128
6010  IFR=1THENW(T)=W(T)+64
6020  IFR=2THENW(T)=W(T)+32
6030  IFR=3THENW(T)=W(T)+16
6040  IFR=4THENW(T)=W(T)+8
6050  IFR=5THENW(T)=W(T)+4
6060  IFR=6THENW(T)=W(T)+2
6070  IFR=7THENW(T)=W(T)+1
6080  RETURN
7000  IFR=0THENE(T)=E(T)+128
7010  IFR=1THENE(T)=E(T)+64
7020  IFR=2THENE(T)=E(T)+32
7030  IFR=3THENE(T)=E(T)+16
7040  IFR=4THENE(T)=E(T)+8
7050  IFR=5THENE(T)=E(T)+4
7060  IFR=6THENE(T)=E(T)+2
7070  IFR=7THENE(T)=E(T)+1
7080  RETURN

READY.
```

```
1 REM**SPRITE CREATION** KEYBOARD VERSION
5 DIMQ(22),W(22),E(22)
10 PRINT"◌":SC=1024:A=0:B=0:CL=55296
11 PRINT"█████████████████████████████◤─────
    ──────"
12 PRINT"█████████████████████████████◤SPRITE
   CREATER─"
13 PRINT"█████████████████████████████◤─────
    ──────"
14 PRINT"█████████████████████████████◤'Q'
   TO RE-RUN.."
15 PRINT"█████████████████████████████◤'F5'
   TO RUBOUT.."
16 PRINT"█████████████████████████████◤'F7'
   TO SKETCH.."
17 PRINT"█████████████████████████████◤'RETURN
   DATA.."
20 GETA$
30 IFA$="Q"THENGOTO10
40 IFA$="◌"THENB=B-1
50 IFA$="◌"THENB=B+1
60 IFA$="◌"THENA=A-1
70 IFA$="◌"THENA=A+1
80 IFA$=CHR$(13)THENGOTO2000
81 IFA$="◌"THENZ=1
82 IFA$="◌"THENZ=0
90 IFB<0THENB=0
100 IFB>20THENB=20
110 IFA<0THENA=0
120 IFA>23THENA=23
130 IFZ=0THENPOKESC+A+40*B,32:FORT=1TO30
    :NEXT:POKESC+A+40*B,160:POKECL+A+40
    *B,1
131 IFZ=1THENPOKESC+A+40*B,160:POKECL+A+
    40*B,13:FORT=1TO30:NEXT:POKESC+A+40
    *B,32
```

111

```
 140 GOTO20
2000 REM********
2010 REM*DECODE*
2020 REM********
2021 PRINT"███████████████████████████████
     ███STAGE# 1"
2030 FORT=1TO21
2031 IFT=1THEN2090
2032 SC=SC+40
2090 FORR=0TO7
2100 IFPEEK(SC+R)=160THENGOSUB5000
2110 NEXT
2120 NEXT
2121 PRINT"███████████████████████████████
     ███STAGE# 2"
2130 SC=1032
2140 FORT=1TO21:IFT=1THEN2160
2150 SC=SC+40
2160 FORR=0TO7
2170 IFPEEK(SC+R)=160THENGOSUB6000
2180 NEXT
2190 NEXT
2191 PRINT"███████████████████████████████
     ███FINAL STAGE"
2200 SC=1040
2210 FORT=1TO21:IFT=1THEN2230
2220 SC=SC+40
2230 FORR=0TO7
2240 IFPEEK(SC+R)=160THENGOSUB7000
2250 NEXT
2260 NEXT
2265 GOTO2341
2270 PRINT"□————————————————————————————
     ————————————                        DATA"
2280 PRINT"—————————————————————————————
     ——————————"
```

112

```
2290 PRINT"DO YOU WANT TO SEND THE DATA
     TO THE      [P][PRINTER OR [N][WRITE IT
     DOWN"
2291 INPUTA$:IFA$="P"THENOPEN4,4:CMD4
2300 PRINT"[]":FORT=1TO21
2310 PRINT"DATA"Q(T)","W(T)","E(T)
2320 NEXT
2322 IFA$="P"THENPRINT#4:CLOSE4:PRINT"[]"
2330 PRINT"[S]HIT 'RETURN' TO CONTINUE"
2339 GETA$:IFA$<>CHR$(13)THEN2339
2340 GOTO2350
2341 PRINT"[]WOULD YOU LIKE TO VIEW YOUR
     SPRITE"
2342 INPUTA$:IFA$="Y"THEN3000
2343 GOTO2270
2350 PRINT"[]WOULD YOU LIKE TO CREATE
     ANOTHER SPRITE"
2351 FORN=0TO62:POKE832+N,0:NEXT:N=0
2360 INPUTA$:IFA$="Y"THENRUN
2362 IFA$="N"THEN2370
2366 GOTO10
2370 PRINT"[]YOU HAVE BEEN USING THE
     'SPRITE CREATER'":END
3000 V=53248:POKEV+21,4:POKE2042,13
3002 D=832:POKEV+23,0:POKEV+29,0
3003 POKEV+4,200:POKEV+5,200
3010 FORTT=1TO21
3020 POKED,Q(TT):POKED+1,W(TT):POKED+2,
     E(TT):D=D+3:NEXT
3050 PRINT"[]DO YOU WANT YOUR SPRITE
     ENLARGED"
3051 INPUTA$:IFA$="Y"THENPOKEV+23,4:
     POKEV+29,4
3055 PRINT"[]"
3059 FORX=0TO200:POKEV+4,X:POKEV+5,X:
     NEXT
```

113

```
3060 PRINT"☐HIT 'RETURN' TO CONTINUE"
3070 GETA$:IFA$< >CHR$(13)THEN3070
3080 GOTO2270
5000 IFR=0THENQ(T)=Q(T)+128
5010 IFR=1THENQ(T)=Q(T)+64
5020 IFR=2THENQ(T)=Q(T)+32
5030 IFR=3THENQ(T)=Q(T)+16
5040 IFR=4THENQ(T)=Q(T)+8
5050 IFR=5THENQ(T)=Q(T)+4
5060 IFR=6THENQ(T)=Q(T)+2
5070 IFR=7THENQ(T)=Q(T)+1
5080 RETURN
6000 IFR=0THENW(T)=W(T)+128
6010 IFR=1THENW(T)=W(T)+64
6020 IFR=2THENW(T)=W(T)+32
6030 IFR=3THENW(T)=W(T)+16
6040 IFR=4THENW(T)=W(T)+8
6050 IFR=5THENW(T)=W(T)+4
6060 IFR=6THENW(T)=W(T)+2
6070 IFR=7THENW(T)=W(T)+1
6080 RETURN
7000 IFR=0THENE(T)=E(T)+128
7010 IFR=1THENE(T)=E(T)+64
7020 IFR=2THENE(T)=E(T)+32
7030 IFR=3THENE(T)=E(T)+16
7040 IFR=4THENE(T)=E(T)+8
7050 IFR=5THENE(T)=E(T)+4
7060 IFR=6THENE(T)=E(T)+2
7070 IFR=7THENE(T)=E(T)+1
7080 RETURN

READY.
```